TABLE OF CONTENTS

PREFACE

Core Communication: A Guide to Organizational Assessment, Planning and Improvement provides an integrated approach to assessment, planning and improvement, drawing on the framework of the Malcolm Baldrige Program of the National Institute of Standards and Technology (NIST, 2006). The Baldrige framework is widely acknowledged as one of the most useful and influential organizational assessment models ever developed.

The Baldrige criteria offer the best available standards of effectiveness for organizations of all kinds. This book aims to provide a synthesis of the perspective and language of this robust framework as applied to communication organizations. The approach stresses the importance of organizational leadership, effectiveness, assessment, continuous improvement, strategic planning, performance and outcomes measurement. An underlying theme is that review, planning and continuous improvement are fundamental to organizational effectiveness and should be thoroughly integrated into the fabric of every organization.

The result is an approach that is extremely useful as a guide to assessment, planning and improvement throughout a communication organization—be it a consulting group, an internal or an external communication function. This approach is equally helpful for entire organizations or components of a larger organization. Having a common framework for assessment, planning and improvement can be of great value in advancing the effectiveness of individual units, and in creating a more integrated and effective overall organization.

The Malcolm Baldrige National Quality Award (MBNQA) program was established by the U.S. Congress in 1987. Named after Secretary of Commerce Malcolm Baldrige, who served from 1981 until his death in 1987, the intent of the program is to promote U.S. business effectiveness for the advancement of the national economy by providing a systems approach to organizational assessment and improvement. More specifically, the goals of the program are to:

▸ Identify the essential components of organizational excellence.

▸ Recognize organizations that demonstrate these characteristics.

▸ Promote information sharing by exemplary organizations.

▸ Encourage the adoption of effective organizational principles and practices.

The program, which is administered by the National Institute for Standards and Technology (NIST), has also been influential in national and international efforts to identify and encourage the application of core principles of organizational excellence. The number of state, local and regional awards programs based on the Baldrige criteria increased from eight programs in 1991 to 43 programs in 1999 (Calhoun, 2002; Vokurka, 2001), and by 1991, over 25 different countries had used the Baldrige criteria as the basis for their own national award (Przasnyski & Tai, 2002). Subsequently, this number has increased to over 60 national awards in other countries (Vokurka, 2001). One example is the European Foundation Quality Model.[1]

---

[1] For more information, see the EQFM web site at http://www.efqm.org/Default.aspx?tabid=35.

The Baldrige model has been an extremely popular framework for organizational self-assessment. NIST estimates that thousands of organizations have used the criteria for this purpose (Calhoun, 2002). There is also evidence that, from a financial perspective, MBNQA winning organizations outperform other organizations. Przasnyski and Tai's (2002) analysis demonstrates that organizations that have been recognized as leaders by Baldrige perform well in the marketplace and, specifically, that "companies derive the most benefit, through evaluating and responding to the [Baldrige] guidelines" (p. 486). In addition, there is evidence that these organizations excel in both growth and profits.

Further evidence suggests that the Baldrige program provides a valuable gauge of organizational effectiveness. A study by the Government Accountability Office of 20 companies that scored high in the Baldrige process found that these results corresponded with increased job satisfaction, improved attendance, reduced turnover, improved quality, reduced cost, increased reliability, increased on-time delivery, fewer errors, reduced lead time (customers), improved satisfaction, fewer complaints, higher customer retention rates (profitability), improved market share and improved financial indicators (Heaphy & Gruska, 1995.) In sum, there is a good deal of evidence to suggest that organizations scoring well on Baldrige standards are more successful than others, providing support for assertions that the Baldrige criteria provide a standard of excellence to which organizations can and should aspire.

From this evidence, it follows that Baldrige-based self-assessment is a useful step toward communication effectiveness. Baldrige-based assessment can be helpful in attaining a variety of organizational development goals, including:

▶ Fostering organizational self-reflection.

▶ Educating participants about dimensions of organizational excellence.

▶ Team-building.

▶ Increasing and enhancing communication.

▶ Professional development.

▶ Promoting comparisons.

▶ Identifying improvement needs.

▶ Providing a model of organizational excellence.

▶ Benchmarking.

▶ Performance measurement.

▶ Leadership development.

This publication owes a debt of gratitude to the Baldrige program; to colleagues at Rutgers University with whom we've worked to adapt the framework to the specialized needs of higher education, student organizations and other contexts; and to fellow IABC professionals whose work is cited at various points in this publication (see "Works Cited and Suggested Readings"). We offer special thanks to Heather Turbeville and IABC for their encouragement and support for this project, their helpful feedback and suggestions, and their guidance throughout the book publishing process.

INTRODUCTION

**PERSONAL AND PROFESSIONAL LEARNING IN COMMUNICATION ORGANIZATIONS:
BENEFITS OF THE ASSESSMENT, PLANNING AND IMPROVEMENT PROCESS /** Anyone
who has worked in a professional communication organization knows that assessment, planning and improvement processes should come first. However, as most communication professionals can attest, in practice, these important processes often come last, if at all.

All too often, those paying our salaries and making promotion decisions also have great
difficulty stepping back from the everyday chaos to set aside the time it takes to undertake
these assessment, planning and improvement activities. And yet, we all know that taking a
"time out" to assess and plan can increase not only an individual's effectiveness but also the
effectiveness of a person's work group and the larger organization of which he or she is a
part. *Core Communication* is designed to provide a simple and straightforward tool for help-
ing communication professionals achieve these benefits with a minimum amount of pain.

Core Communication is designed for the full range of communication organizations: consulting, employee (internal), stakeholder and consumer (external). It is appropriate for
communication professionals in any industry—for example, a corporate communication
unit; a communication department within a university; a governmental office of communication; or a communication organization within a hospital, manufacturing or health care
environment.

An important characteristic of *Core Communication* is its flexibility. That means that *Core
Communication* can be used for an entire communication organization or a department or
work group within such an organization. The *Core Communication* model is well suited for
use in organizational self-assessment for a wide variety of communication organizations, and
can be used to assist with reviews from governing bodies and international associations as
well as internal communication audits (for more information on communication audits, see
www.iabc.com). The program can be used as the basis for program or departmental work-
shops, planning sessions and retreats; for peer review or external audits; or for departmental
self-assessment. In addition, the *Core Communication* process is designed so that all members of a communication organization—regardless of their level within the organization—
will have an opportunity to meaningfully participate in, and learn from, the program.

Having a common model, adaptable for use in so many diverse ways throughout the organization, can be extremely helpful in promoting a shared vision and shared standards of
excellence. Moreover, *Core Communication* facilitates communication and the sharing of
effective practice approaches and outcomes that, in turn, increase the possibility of ongoing
collaboration between and within departments.

Core Communication focuses on seven categories that are important to the functioning
of communication organizations. For each category, the guide poses a number of specific
questions to assist with the review, planning and improvement process.

Collectively, the framework provides a structure for analyzing the workings of communication organizations, with the goal of generating insights that will be helpful for determining

how effectively the organization is functioning today, identifying strengths that can be leveraged, and identifying priorities and developing action plans for areas that would benefit from improvement.

Core Communication is designed to contribute to the process of reflective learning. Reflective learning is essential to the way in which communication professionals build upon and improve our products, programs, services and associated processes. Upon completion of a project, the skilled communication professional takes time to assess the project in terms of what went wrong as well as what went right. From here, the communication professional uses this newfound knowledge to build upon and improve the project going forward. This is precisely the same reflective learning process that is fostered through participation in the *Core Communication* process, although in this case the focus is the communication organization, rather than specific communication products, programs, or services and their associated processes. Regardless of the communicator's experience or current status (entry level, specialist, manager), participation in the *Core Communication* program will enhance his or her understanding of the components of effective organizations, and the strengths and improvement opportunities within his or her organization. It will also enhance personal skills in leadership, strategic planning and assessment.

Benefits of the *Core Communication* approach include:

▶ Providing a well-established framework for organizational review, planning and improvement in communication organizations.

▶ Creating baseline measures and a standard of comparison using an accepted assessment framework.

▶ Sharpening the focus on the needs, expectations, perspectives and satisfaction/dissatisfaction levels of the employees of a communication organization and groups served by that organization or its activities, products, programs, or services and associated processes.

▶ Highlighting and clarifying organizational strengths.

▶ Identifying and prioritizing potential areas for improvement.

▶ Providing a common language and shared framework for discussing and analyzing communication organizations.

▶ Facilitating information sharing and helpful comparisons within and across committees and organizations.

▶ Providing a constructive response to requests for increased accountability.

▶ Enhancing organizational knowledge and skill among organizational members.

▶ Broadening awareness of issues related to organizational leadership and effectiveness.

In addition to achieving the core purposes of *Core Communication*—assessment, planning and improvement—there are a number of benefits from the process, such as: leadership development, team-building, heightening employee engagement, creating focus, identifying strengths, and learning about other employees and their perspectives on the organization.

CHALLENGES FACING COMMUNICATION ORGANIZATIONS / Communication organizations face a number of challenges and pressures that point to the need for a systematic approach to assessment, planning and improvement:

1. **Managing information overload and being sure the right people have the right information when they need it most.**[2] In today's era of instant messaging, text messaging, web site technology and blogs, the professional communicator (and, indeed, each employee) has an added responsibility to filter through a ton of information to find what's relevant to the task at hand. Communication organizations can help by providing guidelines that encourage staff to make the best use of e-mail, voice mail and other types of media. In addition, they can help by ensuring that timely and relevant information is pushed to employees as it's needed. These aspects will be considered as a part of the information sharing section of the *Core Communication* process.

2. **Measuring ROI of internal communication.** A great deal of money is invested in internal and external communication within firms and agencies of many varieties. How are leaders in those organizations to know whether those resources are being wisely invested? Unfortunately, there is a shortage of templates and examples available to help professional communicators answer this question. Because it provides a systematic framework for review, planning and assessment, the *Core Communication* process becomes very useful as a hands-on tool to aid the professional communicator in responding to this challenge.

3. **Sustaining credibility.** Here the challenge is not only what is said, but also how it is said. Collaboration and information sharing are contagious. They thrive in an environment when they are encouraged and rewarded. The heart of the *Core Communication* process reinforces this value. In fact, the process itself relies heavily on collaboration and sharing, encouraging participants in the process to share their insights, observations and perspectives for the betterment of the organization as a whole.

4. **Working with limited resources.** In all organizations, there are limits to the amount of funding and/or resources—be it people, equipment or services—that can be provided to each department. Operating effectively with restricted resources requires careful review and priority setting. We've all experienced situations where one department continues to receive additional funding and resources while other departments do not. In most instances this is due to the well-defined missions, focus and goals of the more prosperous department.

---

[2] Numbers 1–4 based on a list included in Weiner, M. (2005). "Putting best practices into practice." *Communication World* 22(4), 24–27.

Programs, groups and organizations viewed as functioning effectively, maintaining high standards, providing strong leadership and vigorously pursuing improvements also find greater support from their members and the organization. For the effective communication professional, this means that "doing more with less" has become a requirement, and it is now essential to clarify priorities and focus attention on the most critical tasks.

5. Learning from the effective practices of other communication organizations and from organizations in other sectors and industries.[3] Although there are unique roles within the communication organization, its members can still benefit from effective organizations of all kinds—both those specializing in communication and those with other specialties. The communication organization must explore the similarities as well as the differences between its organization and other effective organizations by looking at existing programs and activities in new ways. *Core Communication* promotes this kind of broad and creative thinking.

6. Preparing members to lead. Leadership is a necessity at every level within every organization. It is just as important for an entry-level communication generalist to effectively manage his or her projects as it is for the department manager to successfully lead the entire department. In most instances, leadership qualities are developed through hard work, reflection, active learning and practice—all of which can be aided through professional development opportunities. The challenge is to clarify the knowledge and skills necessary for effective communication leadership, and then to create opportunities to attract, develop and reward members with such capabilities. A vision of what constitutes an effective organization and successful leadership, a commitment to institutional self-reflection, and the competencies necessary to ensure collaborative and continuous improvement are among the key elements needed for the excellence in leadership that is so much in demand—and all of these capabilities are encouraged by the *Core Communication* model.

7. Making accountability an opportunity. Within most organizations, demands for greater accountability and outcomes measurement are increasing. Examples of this have been noted most recently where budget allocations are becoming linked to performance and accountability measures. Developing meaningful criteria for assessing excellence, and using those criteria to measure and track an organization's achievements and outcomes and to inform decision making and resource allocation, is an increasing necessity. However, it can also be an opportunity. Too much delay in addressing these issues is likely to result in performance criteria being defined and imposed by outside individuals and groups who may have less inclusive views of what should be measured, and how it should be done.

8. Adopting a higher standard of excellence. The communication professionals who comprise IABC have agreed to a code of ethics and are held to a high personal standard. *Core Communication* focuses on organizational standards and calls upon professional communicators to adopt and promote a broad and inclusive approach to excellence that leads us to aspire to exemplary practices in all facets of organizational functioning.

---

[3] Numbers 5–6 based on a list included in (2003). "Proving Your Worth." *Communication World, 20*(3), 34–36.

9.   Integrating approaches to assessment, planning and continuous improvement.
While the professional communicator knows that assessment and planning are priorities,
most in practice primarily focus their efforts on implementation. As noted previously,
there are relatively few assessment and planning models available. *Core Communication* is
designed to help address the need for new assessment, planning and improvement frame-
works, and for the application of these models to address the challenges and opportunities
confronting communication organizations.

**10. Bridging the gap between communication specialists and others within the orga-
nization.** Professional communicators have specialized training, roles and responsibilities,
as do engineers, sales and marketing personnel, and computing specialists. To be effective,
it is necessary to communicate and interact successfully with those in other specialties, roles
and departments. One of the challenges is to adopt approaches that encourage interaction and consultation, but that also ensure the commitment to timely decision making and
change is not simply rhetorical. If this does not happen, silos will be reinforced, performance
will diminish, and the entire organization will suffer. Another challenge is to gain trust
from senior leadership so that the communication function can effectively oversee, coach
and counsel all organizational communications. This will allow for a strong, consistent
voice to come from within the organization. One of the greatest advantages of being a
communication professional that is easily overlooked is the role we play in connecting and
linking the various roles and units within the organization. *Core Communication* recognizes
and encourages the importance of this function.

CHAPTER I /
An Integrated Approach to Assessment, Planning, Continuous Improvement and Leadership

MAKING THE BEST USE OF THIS GUIDEBOOK / *Core Communication* was developed to address many of the needs confronting communication organizations—particularly those over which we can exercise direct influence.

The goal of this publication is to offer a comprehensive guide to review, planning and continuous improvement for communicators and their organizations. The process emphasizes the importance of:

▶ Broadly defining effectiveness.

▶ Valuing leadership and planning.

▶ Establishing clear, shared and measurable goals.

▶ Creating effective programs and departments.

▶ Conducting systematic assessments of outcomes.

▶ Engaging in comparisons with peers and leaders.

As shown in Figure 1, the most fundamental characteristic of the process is a commitment to an iterative process of mission-based goal setting, assessment and improvement.

FIGURE 1. CORE PRINCIPLES OF THE BALDRIGE-BASED FRAMEWORK

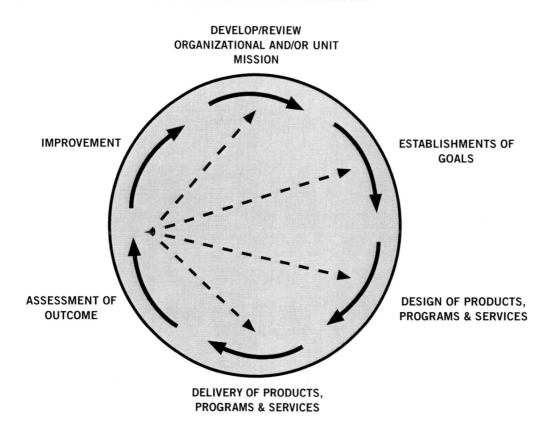

The framework draws on elements used in management audits, disciplinary reviews and strategic planning to provide a generic model with a common language for use across all functions and levels of an organization. See Figure 2.

FIGURE 2. COMMUNICATION ORGANIZATION REVIEW AND IMPROVEMENT APPROACHES

BALDRIGE ASSESSMENT
EXTERNAL REVIEW
PROGRAM ASSESSMENT
MANAGEMENT AUDIT
STRATEGIC PLANNING BASICS

CORE COMMUNICATION:
A GUIDE
TO
ORGANIZATIONAL
ASSESSMENT,
PLANNING AND
IMPROVEMENT

A LEADER'S GUIDE / *Core Communication* is both a theoretical and practical handbook for leaders and planners at all levels. While it does not offer a "how-to" manual for strategic planning or leadership, it does offer a systematic and integrated vision of organizational effectiveness and a checklist of key areas to be considered in determining where a communication program, department or organization stands in relation to that vision. In so doing, it establishes a foundation that is essential for effective leadership, planning and improvement and that can be used by any communication unit.

THE FRAMEWORK AND REVIEW PROCESS / CORE CONCEPTS AND VALUES

The *Core Communication* framework and review process focuses on elements that are essential to establishing and maintaining an outstanding communication program, department or organization. The framework assumes a particular set of organizational concepts and values, which it implicitly promotes throughout:

▶ A clear sense of purpose (mission) and future aspirations (vision) broadly shared, understood and valued.

▶ Effective leadership at all levels, including mechanisms for feedback and review.

▶ Strategic plans, priorities and goals to translate purposes and aspirations into specific products, programs, services, activities and associated processes to ensure that operations and resources are effectively and efficiently used in support of these directions.

▶ High-quality communication products, programs, services and their associated processes, consistent with the established mission and aspirations, carefully designed, regularly evaluated and continuously improved.

▶ Information about the needs, expectations and experiences of key constituencies. This information should be gathered and used as input to product, program, service and associated process development; review and improvement; and to guide day-to-day decision making.

▶ Strong and mutually valued relationships with constituencies, particularly with those individuals and groups who benefit most directly from the products, programs, services and associated processes offered by the department or organization.

▶ Qualified and dedicated employees and a satisfying work environment, with ongoing review and improvement as priorities.

▶ Systematic review processes and the assessment of outcomes to document current strengths; clarity of areas in need of improvement; determination of how successfully the program, department or organization is fulfilling its mission and aspirations; and assessment and improvement of the effectiveness of products, programs, services and associated processes.

▶ Comparisons with peers and leaders for review and improvement.

The *Core Communication* framework is built on the assumption that whether the focus is a communication program, team, work group, department or an entire firm, the foregoing concepts and values are equally appropriate as standards of excellence. It also assumes that these standards are useful as criteria for organizational review, and as a guide for leaders when it comes to guiding planning and improvement efforts.

Structurally, the *Core Communication* framework, illustrated in Figure 3, is composed of questions grouped into seven major categories:[4]

1. Leadership

2. Strategic planning

3. Beneficiaries and constituencies

4. Products, programs, services and associated processes

5. Employee satisfaction and workplace climate

6. Assessment and information use

7. Outcomes and achievements

FIGURE 3. *CORE COMMUNICATION* FRAMEWORK

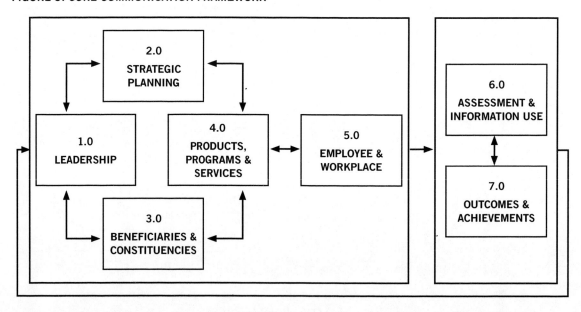

[4] The *Core Communication* model differs somewhat from the Baldrige framework in the terminology used and concepts emphasized. There are also differences in category sequence. Throughout, this guide uses language, concepts and examples that are tailored specifically to communication organizations, whereas Baldrige is generic. Organizationally, this model addresses assessment and information-sharing issues in Category 6, whereas the Baldrige framework considers those concepts in Category 4. See http://baldrige.nist.gov/Criteria.htm.

The *Core Communication* framework is built on the assumption that whether the focus is a communication program, team, work group, department or an entire firm, the foregoing concepts and values are equally appropriate as standards of excellence. It also assumes that these standards are useful as criteria for organizational review, and as a guide for leaders when it comes to guiding planning and improvement efforts.

Structurally, the *Core Communication* framework, illustrated in Figure 3, is composed of questions grouped into seven major categories:[4]

1. Leadership

2. Strategic planning

3. Beneficiaries and constituencies

4. Products, programs, services and associated processes

5. Employee satisfaction and workplace climate

6. Assessment and information use

7. Outcomes and achievements

FIGURE 3. *CORE COMMUNICATION* FRAMEWORK

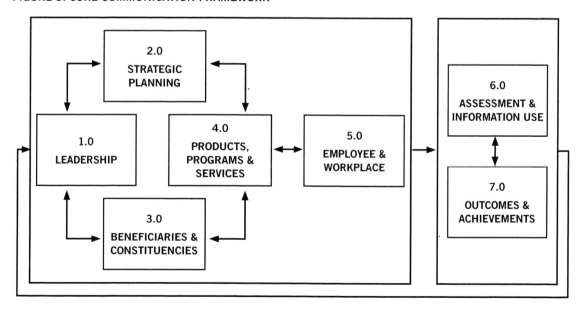

---

[4] The *Core Communication* model differs somewhat from the Baldrige framework in the terminology used and concepts emphasized. There are also differences in category sequence. Throughout, this guide uses language, concepts and examples that are tailored specifically to communication organizations, whereas Baldrige is generic. Organizationally, this model addresses assessment and information-sharing issues in Category 6, whereas the Baldrige framework considers those concepts in Category 4. See http://baldrige.nist.gov/Criteria.htm.

A LEADER'S GUIDE / *Core Communication* is both a theoretical and practical handbook for leaders and planners at all levels. While it does not offer a "how-to" manual for strategic planning or leadership, it does offer a systematic and integrated vision of organizational effectiveness and a checklist of key areas to be considered in determining where a communication program, department or organization stands in relation to that vision. In so doing, it establishes a foundation that is essential for effective leadership, planning and improvement and that can be used by any communication unit.

THE FRAMEWORK AND REVIEW PROCESS / CORE CONCEPTS AND VALUES

The *Core Communication* framework and review process focuses on elements that are essential to establishing and maintaining an outstanding communication program, department or organization. The framework assumes a particular set of organizational concepts and values, which it implicitly promotes throughout:

▸ A clear sense of purpose (mission) and future aspirations (vision) broadly shared, understood and valued.

▸ Effective leadership at all levels, including mechanisms for feedback and review.

▸ Strategic plans, priorities and goals to translate purposes and aspirations into specific products, programs, services, activities and associated processes to ensure that operations and resources are effectively and efficiently used in support of these directions.

▸ High-quality communication products, programs, services and their associated processes, consistent with the established mission and aspirations, carefully designed, regularly evaluated and continuously improved.

▸ Information about the needs, expectations and experiences of key constituencies. This information should be gathered and used as input to product, program, service and associated process development; review and improvement; and to guide day-to-day decision making.

▸ Strong and mutually valued relationships with constituencies, particularly with those individuals and groups who benefit most directly from the products, programs, services and associated processes offered by the department or organization.

▸ Qualified and dedicated employees and a satisfying work environment, with ongoing review and improvement as priorities.

▸ Systematic review processes and the assessment of outcomes to document current strengths; clarity of areas in need of improvement; determination of how successfully the program, department or organization is fulfilling its mission and aspirations; and assessment and improvement of the effectiveness of products, programs, services and associated processes.

▸ Comparisons with peers and leaders for review and improvement.

Categories 1 through 5 focus on factors that contribute to organizational effectiveness. Category 6 addresses issues associated with assessment and review in order to provide documentation of outcomes and achievements—the topic of Category 7. As suggested by the arrows, assessment and outcomes information from categories 6 and 7 are also vital input for leadership, planning, products/programs/services/processes, and employee/workplace considerations. Thus, each of the seven categories represents a critical component of a complex and highly interdependent system that is characteristic of any communication organization.

THE REVIEW PROCESS

The review process consists of a category-by-category review of each of the seven major areas. The review "freezes" the ongoing dynamics of an organization, focusing on each component one at a time to highlight the strengths and potential areas for improvement of the department or organization in that area.

A common characteristic of categories 1 through 6 is that they focus on issues of *approach* and *implementation*, while the focus of Category 7 is on *outcomes*. *Approach* refers to the methods and strategies used. *Implementation* refers to the manner and extent to which approaches are applied and enacted within an organization. *Outcomes* refers to evidence of results, accomplishments and achievements.

GETTING STARTED / Ideally, the entire organization would have the opportunity to complete all seven categories of the *Core Communication* framework in the review process. As noted earlier, one good way to accomplish this is to conduct the *Core Communication* program during a one or two-day retreat or workshop. However, an advantage of this model over other organizational assessment methods is that it can be used in a variety of different formats. Some organizations, for example, may find it difficult to complete the program all at once. In such an instance, the unit could choose to undertake the review in a more segmented way, completing one or more categories at a time, perhaps as a part of a special series of breakfast or lunch sessions, or as a part of regular monthly meetings.

Another useful approach would be to select categories based on pressing issues or challenges the organization faces. An individual program work group, team, department or organization can pursue a variety of options to address its particular concerns. The following represents suggestions as to how this might work.

Issue: Need to sharpen organizational purpose, vision or focus.

Initial categories to complete: *Leadership, Strategic Planning, Assessment and Information Use*

Issue: Need to review or prioritize products, programs, services or processes.

Initial categories to complete: *Beneficiaries and Constituencies; Assessment and Information Use; Products, Programs, Services and Associated Processes*

RESOURCES NEEDED

To insure the maximum benefit from the program, the organization's leadership should allocate an appropriate amount of time for assessment, improvement planning and implementation follow-through. In general, the review and discussion of each category will probably require one to two hours. After the discussion, the group will need to develop an improvement plan to address priorities that are identified. That process may require another hour per category. Additional time is required for actual implementation of the project plans, depending wholly on the extent of plans and the number of people involved.

How to get started:

▸ Determine if you will explore your entire organization or a specific program, work group or team.

▸ Determine if you would like to use the *Core Communication* program in its entirety or in part.

▸ Identify a facilitator (from inside or outside the organization) to lead the process.

▸ Schedule a meeting with organizational leadership to discuss *Core Communication*, its purpose, goals and anticipated outcomes.

▸ Identify and determine what you want to learn about your organization, and where in general, you think improvement is needed.

CHAPTER 2/ Components of the *Core Communication* Framework

THE ORGANIZATIONAL OVERVIEW AND PROFILE / Preceding the seven assessment categories is a section titled "Communication Organization Overview and Profile." Included in this section are questions that call for a generic description of the communication organization, department, work group, team or program to be reviewed—its structure, key constituencies and other characteristics, as noted in the outline in Figure 4.

FIGURE 4. CATEGORIES AND ITEMS

0.0 Communication Organization Overview and Profile
    0.1 Mission, structure and employees
    0.2 Products, programs, services and constituencies
    0.3 Peers and competitors
    0.4 Challenges and opportunities

1.0 Leadership
    1.1 Organizational leadership
    1.2 Public and professional leadership
    1.3 Ethics and social responsibility

2.0 Strategic Planning
    2.1 Plan development
    2.2 Plan implementation

3.0 Beneficiaries and Constituencies
    3.1 Needs and expectations
    3.2 Relationship enhancement

4.0 Products, Programs, Services and Associated Processes
    4.1 Mission-critical products, programs, services and associated processes
    4.2 Operational and support services and processes

5.0 Employee Satisfaction and Workplace Climate
    5.1 Employee satisfaction
    5.2 Workplace climate

6.0 Assessment and Information Use
    6.1 Assessment approach and methods
    6.2 Comparative analysis
    6.3 Information sharing and use

7.0 Outcomes and Achievements
    7.1 Leadership
    7.2 Strategic planning
    7.3 Beneficiaries and constituencies
    7.4 Products, programs, services and associated processes
    7.5 Employee satisfaction and workplace climate
    7.6 Assessment and information use

THE CATEGORIES AND CONCEPTS / CATEGORY 1 – LEADERSHIP

Category 1 considers leadership approaches used to guide the communication organization, department or program; how leaders and leadership practices encourage effectiveness, innovation and attention to the needs of individuals, groups and/or organizations that benefit from the products, programs, services and associated processes of the organization, department or program; and how leadership practices are reviewed and improved.

CATEGORY 2 – STRATEGIC PLANNING

The strategic planning category considers how the mission, vision and values of the organization, department or program are developed and communicated; how they are translated into goals and plans; and how employees are engaged in those activities. Also considered are the ways in which goals and plans are translated into action and coordinated throughout the organization.

CATEGORY 3 – BENEFICIARIES AND CONSTITUENCIES

The beneficiaries and constituencies category focuses on the groups that benefit from the products, programs, services and associated processes offered by the communication program, department or organization being reviewed. The category asks how the organization learns about the needs, perceptions and priorities of those groups, and how that information is used to enhance the organization's reputation and working relationships with those constituencies.

CATEGORY 4 – PRODUCTS, PROGRAMS, SERVICES AND ASSOCIATED PROCESSES

Category 4 focuses on the products, programs, services and associated processes offered by the communication organization, department or program under review, and how their effectiveness is maintained and enhanced. The most important operational and support services are also reviewed.

CATEGORY 5 – EMPLOYEE SATISFACTION AND WORKPLACE CLIMATE

Category 5 considers how the communication program, department or organization being reviewed recruits and retains employees, encourages effectiveness and engagement, creates and maintains a positive workplace culture and climate, and promotes and facilitates personal and professional development.

CATEGORY 6 – ASSESSMENT AND INFORMATION USE

The assessment and information use category focuses on how the program, department or organization assesses its efforts to fulfill its mission and aspirations. Toward this end, the assessment focuses on all facets of organizational effectiveness. Also considered is how assessment information is used for improvement of the organization and its functioning.

CATEGORY 7 – OUTCOMES AND ACHIEVEMENTS

Examining evidence of outcomes and achievements is the theme of Category 7. The category asks for information that documents or demonstrates the quality and effectiveness of the communication program, department or organization.

CHAPTER 3 / Communication Organization Overview and Profile 0.0

Meaningful assessment begins with a high-level description—or overview—of the program, department, or organization and the context in which it operates. This includes descriptions of:

- Mission
- Structure
- Employees
- Major products, programs, services and associated processes
- Key constituencies

Also important is a listing of peers and competitors, leaders in the field, major recommendations from previous internal or external assessments, and key challenges and opportunities facing the organization.

Assembling and formatting this information into a single brief statement is a useful exercise as part of the preparation for a review. That said, completion of the overview is not essential unless the facilitation will be done by persons not intimately familiar with the organization. In that case, the information is vital background to guide the facilitation process. For units that complete the "Overview," the activity can be a helpful way of focusing on high-level characteristics of the organization—characteristics that may make a particular organization similar to that of other communicators, and those that may make it quite unique. Both sets of characteristics can be quite important to meaningful assessment and planning.

0.1 MISSION, STRUCTURE AND EMPLOYEES
Briefly describe the communication organization, department or program that will be the focus of the assessment, including the following:

1. What is the name of the organization,[5] and what is its primary purpose or mission?

2. How is the organization structured?

3. What are the key elements of the leadership structure?

4. Who are the senior leaders, and what are their primary areas of responsibility?

---

[5] The term *organization* is used in a general sense to refer to any level of organization: a company or department, a work group, a team or a project.

5. To whom does the senior leader of the organization report?

6. Does the organization have advisory or governing boards, and if so, what are their roles and responsibilities?

7. How many full- and part-time employees work in the organization? Briefly describe the responsibilities of each employee group. Which groups are members of bargaining units?

8. What are the major facilities, equipment and technologies for which the organization has responsibility?

9. What is the legal, regulatory, licensing and/or accrediting environment in which the organization operates? Briefly describe any mandated standards, review processes, and financial or environmental regulations that may apply.

10. Has the organization participated in self-assessments, external assessments or reviews within the past five years? What were the major conclusions and recommendations, and what, if any, actions have been undertaken in response to those assessments?

0.2 PRODUCTS, PROGRAMS, SERVICES AND CONSTITUENCIES[6]

1. What are the major products, programs and/or services provided by the organization?

2. For what groups does the organization provide communication products, programs and services? What is the approximate size of each of those groups, and what, in general terms, are their expectations and/or requirements?

3. With what other organizations does the organization have formalized collaborative relationships, alliances or partnerships? What are the nature and purposes of each? Briefly describe any key informal relationships with other groups or organizations. With what other organizations or department do interactions occur on a regular basis?

0.3 PEERS AND COMPETITORS

1. What other communication organizations, departments or programs are considered to be peers, competitors or leaders in the field, market or discipline?

2. In terms of overall quality, stature or standing, how does this communication organization compare with peers, competitors or leaders?

---

[6] Constituencies refers to any stakeholder group or organization that is important to the work of a program, department or organization—either because it benefits from, influences or is influenced by the organization. Thus, advisory or regulatory boards, other departments that provide resources or with which you collaborate, or the senior leadership might not be beneficiaries of the work of your organization in the most precise sense of the term, but they would certainly be important constituencies.

3. What are the principal factors that influence the organization's success relative to peers, competitors or leaders?

0.4 CHALLENGES AND OPPORTUNITIES

1. What are the key organizational challenges at this point in time?

2. What special opportunities exist for advancing the quality, stature or standing of the organization, such as increased visibility, access to senior management and increased control over organizationwide communications?

CHAPTER 4 / Leadership 1.0

☐

Few concepts are as widely discussed in the literature of organizations as leadership. While the perspectives on this topic differ considerably from one author to another, there is widespread agreement that leadership is the cornerstone of effectiveness in any organization.

Senior leaders, along with other leaders and supervisors, have the responsibility of guiding the communication program, department or organization in the pursuit of a clear and shared sense of purpose and direction, facilitating the development and implementation of goals and plans, establishing a culture of collaboration and collegiality, inspiring high levels of performance, encouraging high standards of ethical performance, and promoting and modeling these desired organizational outcomes and values through their own behavior. In essence, senior leaders need to enable a shared understanding among themselves, their managers and their employees to assist with achieving goals, and they need to teach other leaders in the organization how to make the organization more effective (Wann, 1999, p. vii).

Exemplary leadership also involves a commitment to the sharing of expertise and experience beyond the boundaries of the organization, through contributions to public, professional and academic communities. It also requires a dedication to high standards of integrity, ethical conduct and social responsibility to ensure that professional communicators represent themselves and their organizations in a legal, ethical and fair manner consistent with the IABC code of ethics (IABC, 2007).

While these responsibilities are central to the duties of the most *senior* leaders, they are largely shared by all leaders in all areas and at all levels. They are fundamental to the work of directors and managers, and to a greater or lesser degree to the activities of chairs of committees or task forces, team leaders and project coordinators.

CHALLENGES OF COMMUNICATION LEADERSHIP / The difficulties facing leaders of communication organizations are daunting. Individuals in leadership roles within the organization must take account of national and local challenges and competition—organizational goals and priorities, a diverse and often seemingly irreconcilable array of stakeholder expectations, new and reformatted technology, space issues, professional development, and the needs of colleagues. Typically, these leaders have limited resources and, often, too few incentives to foster new initiatives or to foster significant change or renewal.

A second—and crucial—challenge for communication leaders is that they are often in a situation where they must coordinate the work of individuals who do not officially report to them. For example, the project manager on a new web site launch might be a member of the communication department. However, there may be members of the team from other sectors of the organization, such as marketing, IT and other units. The project manager is the team leader, and as such, is responsible for the success of the project. To be successful, the team leader must understand the relevant organizational politics and be adept at managing the work of individuals who may not report to him or her. It is here that leadership effectiveness requires particular leadership competencies, a thorough knowledge of the project, an understanding of the organization's culture, and effectiveness at coordinating the work of an array of differing personalities and styles.

Another significant challenge—particularly as it relates to communication leadership—lies in the fact that those who come to leadership positions from professional and technical positions have often received little leadership training for those roles as part of their formal education. Professional education encourages independent thinking and problem solving. Great value is placed on communication knowledge and skill, and the capabilities necessary for guiding one's professional career. In an organizational context, however, leadership effectiveness requires skill in creating consensus around priorities, consultation in thought and action, and an ability to defer or sublimate one's point of view. In these roles, facilitating and coordinating the contributions of others is critical, as is becoming a student of organizational politics and the economics of one's organization and sector. Success ultimately requires that the individual have a "big picture" perspective and focus his or her primary efforts on promoting personal and professional recognition of others' accomplishments—as well as the achievements of the department or the organization—above his or her own.

Last, but not least, the challenge addressed here is that of the scope of communication functionality, visibility, trust and reach within the organization. The most effective organizations provide for a direct link between the communication leader and senior management as well as a method for the communication function to provide an overall strategy behind the organization's communications to their various constituencies. However, many organizations fail to see the direct links between organizational success and the communication function. Seasoned communication leaders have proven themselves effective at addressing this challenge over time and at gaining the trust and respect of senior management. But the road can be long and daunting in many organizations. For the new or veteran communication leader to get to this position, he or she must possess the ability to become a trusted advisor who can focus on improving overall organizational effectiveness within the big picture rather than solely on day-to-day tasks.

How these challenging tasks can be accomplished effectively—and how people with these capabilities can best be identified, developed and appropriately rewarded—is a matter of continuing discussion and the topic of numerous books and articles on the subject of leadership each year. In addition to disciplinary or subject matter expertise and experience, more general capabilities, such as personal, analytic, organizational and communication competencies, are essential (see for example, Bennis, 1997; Collins, 2001; Kouzes & Posner, 1995; Ruben, 2006a, 2006b; Shaffer, 2000; Unseem, 1998).

DIMENSIONS OF LEADERSHIP EFFECTIVENESS / Although there is no simple formula for effectiveness in leadership in communication organizations, many of the most critical dimensions can be enumerated:

▸ Having a well-defined and inclusive vision of organizational effectiveness and the competencies required for its realization.

▸ Creating a shared commitment to the organization's purposes, needs and aspirations, and maintaining a focus on strategic goals and directions to achieve those ends.

▸ Listening carefully to the voices of individuals, groups and organizations that are the potential beneficiaries of the work of the organization, and encouraging colleagues to do likewise.

▸ Fostering a culture wherein ongoing assessment and improvement as well as fact-based decision making, resource allocation and planning are accepted practices.

▸ Developing an integrated system of leadership to encourage effective, responsible and coordinated oversight of communication processes and messages throughout the organization.

▸ Fostering accountability through the establishment of clear goals and the systematic assessment of outcomes.

▸ Encouraging and using feedback on leadership and institutional effectiveness.

▸ Engaging, coaching and motivating colleagues at all levels to contribute to the best of their capabilities.

▸ Promoting teamwork, collaborative problem solving and a sense of community.

▸ Promoting leadership and professional development, and recognizing the values of personal and organizational learning.

▸ Viewing change as a positive and necessary component of organizational effectiveness.

▸ Representing the organization with external groups and organizations effectively.

▸ Maintaining and promoting high standards of professional integrity and ethical and social responsibility.

▸ Learning about and educating colleagues about opportunities and political and economic challenges facing the practice of communication in general, and the organization, department or program, more specifically.

A fundamental tenet of leadership practice is that leaders are most effective when they are personally and visibly engaged in their work in a manner that demonstrates their commitment to particular organizational values and principles. Through their personal actions, leaders have the opportunity to reaffirm the importance of listening to and understanding the perspectives of those served by the organization, engaging and valuing colleagues at all levels, and encouraging coordinated leadership and accountability throughout the organization. Personal involvement, communication and consensus building are important in all organizations.

1.0 LEADERSHIP: KEY REVIEW ISSUES

Leadership review focuses on how leaders:

▸ Strategically guide their communication organization, department or program.

▸ Build and sustain consensus on its mission and future directions.

▸ Promote a focus on the needs and expectations of key constituencies.[7]

▸ Establish an appropriate level of engagement and collaboration in planning and decision making.

Also examined are the approaches senior leaders use to foster effective, engaged and consultative leadership and governance throughout the organization,[8] and how leadership effectiveness is assessed. Finally, the category focuses on the ways in which leaders share their own and the organization's experience and expertise with public and professional groups and how they establish high standards of ethical and social responsibility.

1.1 ORGANIZATIONAL LEADERSHIP: AREAS TO ADDRESS

A. Leadership Structure and Practice

  1. What is the leadership and governance structure of the organization?

▸ What are the formal reporting relationships within the communication organization?

▸ What are the areas of responsibility of those in leadership positions?

▸ Are leadership and governance roles, responsibilities and reporting relationships well documented?

▸ How is information regarding leadership roles, responsibilities and reporting relationships disseminated?[9]

---

[7] *Constituencies* refers to beneficiaries, clients, stakeholders, consumers, audiences, publics, users or customers for which the organization undertakes activities or provides products, programs or services, or which influence or are influenced by the organization. Depending on the organization's mission, such products, programs and services may include communication programs, product marketing campaigns, press releases, instruction, research or scholarship, public service or outreach, administrative support or other functions. The list of constituency groups and organizations could include customers, employees, shareholders, volunteers, suppliers, partners, state and federal funding agencies, institutions of higher education, advisory boards, disciplinary and administrative opinion leaders at other organizations, local and state government, the citizens of the community or state, and other groups. For departments that provide products, programs and services within the organization—such as human resources, employee communication, facilities and computing services—the relevant groups and organizations would be the departments for which the organization provides services. *Constituencies* also refer to departments inside or outside the organization, with which the organization, department or program collaborates. Additional discussion of beneficiaries and constituencies is provided in Category 3.

[8] The term *organization* is used in a general sense to refer to an organization, a department, a work group, a team or a project.

[9] This may include various documents and channels—print or electronic. The documents may include organizational charts, bylaws, charters, descriptions of policies or procedures, operating manuals or comparable materials.

2. Do leadership practices clarify and advance the organization's mission, aspirations and goals?

   ‣ How are leaders personally and visibly involved in promoting the directions, aspirations and values of the communication organization?

   ‣ What leadership approaches are employed to develop shared understanding and commitment to those directions, aspirations, and values among colleagues and external constituencies?

   ‣ How do senior leaders engage others throughout the communication organization in the periodic assessment and review of the organization's stated mission, aspirations and values?

3. What responsibilities do leaders at various levels have relative to:

   ‣ Strategic planning?

   ‣ Resource allocation?

   ‣ Internal communication?

   ‣ External communication and public relations?

   ‣ Outcomes assessment and the use of outcomes information for improvement?

4. What role do senior leaders play in fostering an organizational culture and climate that:

   ‣ Promotes high standards of individual and collective achievement?

   ‣ Values assessment, planning and improvement?

   ‣ Uses data and information to guide decision making and problem solving?

   ‣ Encourages initiative and innovation?

   ‣ Advances personal and organizational learning?

   ‣ Fosters organizational flexibility and agility?

   ‣ Encourages collaboration and teamwork?

   ‣ Values outreach, service and responsiveness to the needs and expectations of groups and organizations for which products, programs and services are provided?

B. Effectiveness Review

1. How is senior leadership effectiveness assessed?

    ▸ How is informal feedback on leadership effectiveness encouraged and used?

    ▸ What formal evaluation procedures are in place to regularly and systematically assess leadership practices and effectiveness?

    ▸ What methods are used, and how are reliability and anonymity ensured?

    ▸ How is information gained from senior leadership reviews used for improving leadership systems and practices?

2. How is leadership and governance effectiveness assessed throughout the organization?

    ▸ How is informal feedback from colleagues solicited and used?

    ▸ What formal, objective and systematic methods are in place for assessing leadership effectiveness at all levels, and how frequently are reviews undertaken?

    ▸ What methods are used, and how are reliability and anonymity ensured?

    ▸ How is information gained from the review of leadership disseminated and used for improving leadership systems and practices?

1.2 PUBLIC AND PROFESSIONAL LEADERSHIP

1. In what ways do senior leaders—and leaders at all levels—share their expertise and experience beyond their own communication program, department or organization through service on committees, projects, task forces or other initiatives of the larger organization?

    ▸ What are the types and extent of participation?

    ▸ How are decisions made regarding appropriate areas for involvement?

    ▸ How is engagement with other departments, groups and organizations encouraged, supported and recognized?

2. How do your senior leaders—and leaders at all levels in your organization—share their leadership, professional and/or technical expertise and experience with public, professional, or community groups or organizations?

    ▸ What are the types and extent of participation?

    ▸ How are decisions made regarding appropriate areas for involvement?

    ▸ How is visibility and engagement with public, professional and/or community groups and organizations encouraged, supported and recognized by leaders?

1.3 ETHICS AND SOCIAL RESPONSIBILITY: AREAS TO ADDRESS

A. Ethics and Integrity

1. Are principles of leadership integrity and ethical behavior clearly defined?

    ▸ How do senior leaders communicate their personal commitment to the highest standards of ethics and integrity?

    ▸ How do senior leaders create awareness of and commitment to those principles and standards among others?

2. How are areas of potential ethical concern identified?[10] What are those areas, and how are high standards of integrity and ethical behavior ensured in each?

    ▸ How are areas of ethical concern clearly defined, as appropriate, for specific constituencies, including colleagues, customers, professional and public organizations, and the general public?

    ▸ What methods are used to ensure that appropriate standards of ethical conduct and integrity are widely disseminated and understood?

    ▸ What procedures are in place to ensure that policies and procedures relative to integrity and ethical standards are periodically reviewed, clarified and updated as appropriate?

    ▸ What mechanisms are in place for monitoring compliance?

B. Social Responsibility

1. What are the legal and regulatory requirements and/or risks associated with the organization's work, and how is conformance with appropriate standards ensured?

2. How does the organization identify and address the current and potential legal, regulatory, or environmental impact of its operations on the community and society?[11]

    ▸ What are the areas of potential impact?

    ▸ How are they addressed in a proactive manner?

[10] Examples might include issues related to proprietary rights for information and work products, confidentiality, appropriate treatment of employees, employment practices relative to family members, potential conflicts of interest, financial practices or vendor relations. The IABC Code of Ethics at http://www.iabc.com/about/code.htm provides a useful guide to relevant issues and standards for professional communicators in these matters.

[11] Examples might include waste management issues, copyright and trademark concerns, personal or property security, substance abuse, driver safety and health risks.

CHAPTER 5 / Strategic Planning 2.0

Planning is a second vital component of programmatic, departmental and organizational effectiveness. The most fundamental purpose of the planning process is the translation of the mission, vision and strategic directions into clear goals and action plans.

In addition, a planning process "helps us make decisions, get things done, provides a framework for our creativity, and keeps our budget solvent!" (Hettinger & Hattori, 2006).

A clear statement of purpose and direction is a prerequisite to effective planning. "The challenge is to develop messages that further people's understanding, commitment, and productivity" (D'Aprix, 1996, p. 50). Typically, a mission statement provides this foundation:

> Mission statements are necessary to bring clarity of focus to members of the organization, to give them an understanding of how what they do is tied to a greater purpose. A mission statement should be a brief, clear statement of the reasons for an organization's existence, its purpose(s), the function(s) it performs, its primary customer base, and the primary methods through which it will fulfill its purpose(s)....It specifies the functional role the organization plays in its environment, indicating scope and direction of the organization's activities. A mission statement helps differentiate you from your competitors. (Potter, 2001, p. 35)

The mission statement for a program, department or organization may identify its future-oriented aspirations or, as is often the case, its vision may be articulated in a separate statement. Whichever approach is taken, the statement or statements should indicate what is unique and distinctive about a particular unit, and for whom its products, programs and services are provided. Some organizations also develop a statement of values or operating principles that is viewed as an important foundational document. In addition, the mission statement tells what is *not* appropriate for an organization, department or program to do. This approach is especially helpful for units who routinely face last-minute requests on projects that fall outside of the scope of work (Potter, 2001).

As illustrated in Figure 5, the planning process often includes an environmental scan to identify current strengths, weaknesses, opportunities and threats. With these formulations as a backdrop, the planning processes progress to the articulation of measurable goals and the strategies and action plans necessary for their attainment (Tromp & Ruben, 2004).[12] For communication organizations, a detailed plan that describes how the communication activities are tied to overall organizational goals, how they will be evaluated and how the results will be used for improvement is particularly critical (Potter, 1999, p. 13). The documented plan integrates all these components, ensures that resources are aligned with strategic priorities, and includes a framework for monitoring progress and evaluating outcomes.

---

[12] For a more detailed discussion of the strategic planning model and framework presented here, see Tromp and Ruben, 2004.

A PLAN AND A PLANNING PROCESS / Strategic planning consists of a *plan* for advancing a program, department or organization that typically includes the steps described above, as well as a planning *process* through which the particulars of the plan are developed and implemented. Minimally, a successful process requires planning, analysis, message dissemination, understanding by beneficiaries and constituencies, implementation, resources, measurement, and evaluation (Potter, 1999). The model below outlines the steps in the typical planning process. For this or other planning models to be effective, careful attention must be paid to leadership, communication and assessment during each stage in the assessment process. See See Tromp and Reuben (2004) for a detailed discussion of these issues.

FIGURE 5. THE STRATEGIC PLANNING PROCESS

MISSION, VISION AND VALUES + COLLABORATORS AND BENEFICIARIES =

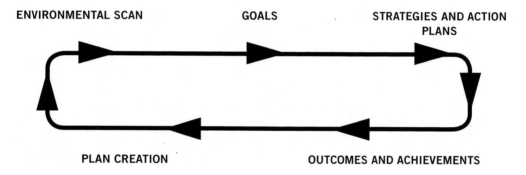

ENVIRONMENTAL SCAN · GOALS · STRATEGIES AND ACTION PLANS

PLAN CREATION · OUTCOMES AND ACHIEVEMENTS

2.0 STRATEGIC PLANNING: KEY REVIEW ISSUES
The strategic planning category focuses on the methods by which a communication organization establishes and reviews its sense of purpose and direction, aspirations, short- and long-term goals, strategies, and action plans for achieving them. Also considered are how employee and/or other constituency group needs and expectations are considered in the planning process, how goals and plans are communicated and coordinated throughout the organization, how progress on goals and plans is assessed, and how follow-through is monitored.

2.1 PLAN DEVELOPMENT: AREAS TO ADDRESS

A. Defined Purpose and Direction

1. Does the communication program, department or organization have a published statement of purpose (mission),[13] aspirations (vision)[14] and broad organizational goals? Are there other published statements or documents addressing values, recommended standards of conduct or operating principles?

2. Do published documents clearly describe the mission, aspirations, beneficiaries and broad organizational goals in a manner that differentiates this organization from others?

3. Do published documents clearly describe products, programs, services and associated processes and make clear their relationship to the mission and vision?

4. Do published documents identify important constituencies?

B. Documented Plans

1. Does the organization have a published strategic plan? How and to whom is the plan disseminated? When was the plan developed?

2. Does the plan define broad organizational goals? Are those goals clearly linked to the mission and vision?

3. How does the plan translate goals into specific strategies and action plans?

4. Are resources aligned with strategic directions?

5. How does the plan take into account issues related to human, fiscal, physical facilities and infrastructure resources?

6. Does the plan specify performance indicators and methods for evaluating progress and outcomes?

C. The Planning Process

1. Is there a formalized planning process?

    ▸ What are the major steps in the process?

    ▸ Are the steps and procedures in the process documented?

---

[13] Mission refers to the primary work of the organization, the purposes for which the organization exists, including specification of the groups for which the organization provides products, programs or services.

[14] Vision refers to a characterization of how the organization sees itself in the future—its broadly expressed, future aspirations—the answer to the question, "What would you like your organization to be like in 10 years?"

▸ How is information about the planning process communicated, and to whom?

▸ How frequently is the planning cycle undertaken?

2. How does the planning process take account of:

   ▸ The mission, vision, values or other foundational documents?

   ▸ The needs and expectations of constituency groups served by the organization?

   ▸ Noteworthy challenges and opportunities?

   ▸ Relevant trends and issues in the field of communication and the region and pertinent considerations related to economics, technology, regulation and the marketplace?

   ▸ Alignment of resources with strategic priorities, including fiscal, human, physical facilities and infrastructure?

   ▸ Organizational capabilities, culture and climate?

3. How is planning linked to assessment and improvement? How does the process consider:

   ▸ Previous organizational assessments, self-studies, internal and/or external reviews, and strategic planning documents?

   ▸ Current assessment outcomes and achievements?[15]

   ▸ Areas in need of improvement?

4. How is broad input and participation in the planning process encouraged?

   ▸ How are employees, customers, board members and/or representatives of other relevant constituency groups engaged in the planning process?

   ▸ What communication approaches and channels are used to keep such groups informed and involved during all stages of the planning process?

5. How is planning coordinated throughout the organization so that the process:

   ▸ Aligns with larger organizational goals?

   ▸ Establishes clear goals, strategies and action steps?

   ▸ Allocates resources in accordance with strategic priorities?

---

[15] Outcomes and achievements refer to the organization's current accomplishments (and those achieved over time) relative to the mission, vision, values, goals and plans, including the quality and effectiveness of programs and services, relationships with the groups and organizations for which it provides programs and/or services or with which it collaborates, employee satisfaction and workplace climate, and organizational effectiveness, more generally. More extensive discussion of these topics is provided in categories 6 and 7.

- ▸ Identifies short- and long-term needs?

- ▸ Clarifies responsibilities and responsible individuals or groups for follow-up?

- ▸ Ensures flexibility to address unplanned and unanticipated events?

- ▸ Takes account of employee professional development and/or training needs?[16]

- ▸ Identifies appropriate performance indicators and methods for monitoring and assessing outcomes?

- ▸ Considers the capabilities and needs of current or potential organizations with which collaboration is important?[17]

- ▸ Considers practices and approaches used by peers, competitors and leaders?[18]

- ▸ Provides a useful resource to leaders at all levels to guide decision making; resource allocation; the development of new products, programs or services and their associated processes; and the modification or termination of products, programs, services and associated processes that are no longer appropriate or effective?

6. How are the mission, vision, goals and plans reviewed, reaffirmed or revised as a part of the planning process to ensure their continuing appropriateness, relevance and usefulness?

7. How often is the planning process itself evaluated and improved, and how is that assessment conducted?

[16] This topic is also addressed in some detail in Category 5.

[17] Organizations with which collaborating is important include all external groups, departments, programs, institutes, organizations or agencies that supply human, physical or financial resources necessary to the work of your organization. For example, colleges and universities are providers of potential employees. Vendors of various types supply goods and services. Also included are other units outside your organization with which you have formed alliances, partnerships, joint programs or shared service arrangements.

[18] Establishing comparisons by considering practices and approaches used by peers, competitors and leaders—also termed benchmarking—refers to the process of identifying, selecting and systematically comparing the organization's performance, products, programs, services, processes, activities, achievements and/or impact with that of other programs, departments and/or organizations. Comparisons may be made with peer and/or competitor organizations and/or with other enterprises that have comparable processes or activities. Comparisons with recognized leaders in the field of communication and/or with leaders in business, health care, higher education or governmental organizations can provide a basis for innovation for your organization.

2.2 PLAN IMPLEMENTATION

1. How are employees and other constituencies, as appropriate, engaged in the implementation of plans?

   ▶ Are roles and responsibilities clearly defined?

   ▶ How are expectations communicated?

2. How is broad dissemination of and access to information about progress on the implementation of plans ensured, and how is shared understanding encouraged?

3. How does the organization follow through on the implementation of its plan to ensure that:

   ▶ Specified goals, strategies and action steps have been appropriately addressed?

   ▶ Alignment between larger organizational and departmental or program goals is achieved?

   ▶ Short- and longer-term needs have been adopted?

   ▶ Implementation responsibilities have been fulfilled?

   ▶ Capabilities and needs of current or potential collaborative organizations have been considered?

   ▶ Professional development and/or training needs have been appropriately taken into account?

   ▶ Performance indicators and methods for monitoring and assessing outcomes are being used?

   ▶ Practices and approaches used by peers, competitors and leaders have been considered?

   ▶ Leaders at all levels are using outcomes of the planning process to guide decision making; resource allocation; the development of new products, programs or services, and their associated processes; and the modification or termination of products, programs, services and associated processes that are no longer appropriate or effective?

4. How do you synchronize, coordinate and oversee the implementation of plans throughout the organization to ensure that:

   ▶ Key internal and external constituencies are informed and appropriately engaged?

   ▶ Resources are allocated in a manner that supports strategic priorities?

   ▶ Unanticipated changes in organizational priorities are taken into consideration?

CHAPTER 6 / Beneficiaries and Constituencies 3.0

Few individuals touch the lives of as many diverse constituencies, directly and indirectly, as communication professionals. Be they employees, shareholders, customers, vendors, community members or the public at large, communication professionals play a truly critical role in creating and maintaining relationships with each group on behalf of their organization.

Like the communication organization as a whole, some departments and programs within it serve external[19] constituency groups, such as vendors, community members and customers. However, some serve primarily internal constituencies, such as employees, other departments or boards. Still others serve both internal and external constituencies.

IDENTIFYING BENEFICIARY AND CONSTITUENCY GROUPS / Communication organizations may differ substantially in the kind of work they do, and for whom they do it. However, the organization as a whole, as well as individual departments, programs, work groups and teams, has a number of beneficiary and constituency groups. Depending on the particular program or department, the list of groups could include one or more of the following:

▸ Those who pay for products, programs or services.

▸ Those who benefit from the organization's products, programs, services or activities.

▸ Those upon whom the organization's existence depends.

▸ Those who can choose to use or not to use the products, programs or services.

▸ Those who provide resources or expertise essential to the work of the organization.

▸ Those whose assessment of the performance of the products, programs, services or activities translates into financial or moral support, or a lack thereof.

BUILDING RELATIONSHIPS WITH BENEFICIARIES AND CONSTITUENCIES / Across all business sectors, the most respected organizations are those that place a great deal of emphasis on understanding the needs, expectations and experiences of those for whom they provide services. They use these insights to form and maintain high quality, mutually beneficial and mutually satisfying relationships with these individuals, groups and organizations. Information from beneficiaries and constituencies is very useful when evaluating current services, communicating about existing services, identifying needed improvements,

---

[19] The term external is used to refer to constituency groups composed of individuals not employed by the institution.

and creating new initiatives. In such organizations, systems are put in place to ensure that those within the program or department have a clear understanding of the experiences of those for whom services are designed to benefit, to clarify their expectations and priorities, to monitor the effectiveness of relationships, to identify and address sources of dissatisfaction that may exist, and more generally to keep in touch with how the organization looks from the "outside" (Baldrige, 2006; Ruben 1995, 2004).

A strong argument can be made for the value of this same approach in communication organizations. Assessment is essential for determining whether the standards of excellence the organization hopes to achieve in its products, programs and services are being translated into reality in the experiences of the intended beneficiaries. Moreover, in a very practical sense, it is clear that external judgments of the quality of a communication program, department or organization translate into the financial and reputational support that is critical to the work and viability of all employees in their respective programs and departments, as well as to the entire organization.

According to Gayeski (2007), "the key to excellent communication is creating the right infrastructure," with one piece of the infrastructure being "the understanding of your...constituent needs" (p. 127). From here, Gayeski says a communication professional will have the resources needed to determine, "what good communication looks like, which projects deserve priority, and how to communicate a consistent organizational voice" (p. 127).

An understanding of the experiences of beneficiary and other constituency groups also helps to identify organizational practices that need improvement, but are easily overlooked by "insiders." For instance, listening to employees or customers may highlight the essential role the "frontline" employees of a program or department play in making their experience a positive one. Employees in these roles are, in effect, the "face of the organization," the first and often the last (and sometimes the only) point of contact. Encounters with frontline employees form the basis of impressions that are remembered and repeated many times. In this case, as in many others that might be mentioned, having a clear sense of the perspectives and needs of beneficiaries helps to clarify factors that are critical if the good intentions of a program, department or organization are to be realized.

How does a communication organization ensure that it has an appropriate focus on beneficiaries and constituencies? Generally speaking, the following steps need to be taken:

1. Identify each group for which the organization provides programs, services, materials or resources.

2. Use interviews, focus groups, surveys and other methods to regularly and systematically gather information from these constituencies to learn about their needs, expectations, priorities, experiences, and sources of satisfaction and dissatisfaction. This assessment should also focus on individuals who *could* benefit from your products, programs and services, but who have made other choices, in order to understand the reasons for their decisions.

3. Analyze information on unmet needs and expectations, sources of dissatisfaction and other gap areas.

4. Address significant gaps by improving products, programs, services and associated processes by using information and education to negotiate new expectations, or by a combination thereof.

In adopting this approach, it is *not* assumed that any communication organization should address each and every beneficiary or constituent need, expectation or concern. Rather, the idea is simply that a better understanding of the perspectives and experiences is essential for the planning and priority-setting process. In a practical sense, failing to gather and use such information is a great disadvantage to any organization in its effort to fulfill its mission and realize its aspirations, and more fundamentally, it seems at odds with the principles of self-reflection, understanding and self-improvement that have long been core values in the field of communication.

3.0 BENEFICIARIES AND CONSTITUENCIES: KEY REVIEW ISSUES

This category considers how a communication program, department or organization learns about the needs, expectations, perspectives, experiences, and satisfaction and dissatisfaction levels of the individuals, groups and organizations for which products, programs and services are provided. Also considered is how this information is analyzed and used to create or refine products, programs or services, and their associated processes, and more generally to enhance relationships and reputation with beneficiary and constituency groups.[20]

3.1 NEEDS AND EXPECTATIONS

1. What groups or organizations benefit most directly from the work of the communication organization, and what products, programs, services and associated processes are provided for each?

---

[20] Beneficiary and constituency groups refers broadly to individuals, groups or organizations—variously termed stakeholders, customers, audiences, users, consumers, clients, audiences or publics—for whom you provide products, programs or services, who benefit directly or indirectly from your work, or who have an important influence on your organization's success. The list of such groups will, of course, depend on the mission of the organization and will be different for profit and nonprofit organizations. Profit groups might include shareholders, customers, vendors, consultants, professional associations, advisory boards, bargaining units, local and state government, the citizens of the community or state, the mass media, and others. In addition to those for-profit groups, nonprofit groups might include volunteers, the public, visitors, families of those that are served, guiding councils, colleges and universities, and many more. Note: Employees are a critical constituency group for all programs, departments and organizations. They are the focus of Category 5 and, therefore, are not considered in this category.

2. What other constituency groups are important to the success of the program?

3. Given the established mission, aspirations, goals and plans, what is the relative priority of each of the beneficiary and constituency[21] groups?

4. How does the communication organization systematically gather information about the pertinent needs, expectations, perspectives, experiences, and sources of satisfaction (or dissatisfaction) of employee and/or other beneficiary and constituency groups?

5. What are the most critical needs and expectations of priority beneficiary and constituency groups?

6. How does the organization listen to and learn about the perspectives and decision making criteria of individuals, groups or organizations that could have chosen your products, programs or services but did not?[22]

7. What information is gathered, analyzed and used to anticipate future needs of the groups and organizations for which products, programs or services are provided? How are the following taken into account:

    ▸ Demographic, technological, competitive, societal, environmental, economic, and regulatory factors and trends?

    ▸ Insights from current, former and potential beneficiary groups or organizations for which you provide products, programs or services, or with which your organization collaborates?

    ▸ Comparisons with peer, competitor and leading programs, departments or organizations?

---

[21] Beneficiaries refers specifically to those individuals, groups and organizations who benefit directly or indirectly from the work of the program, department or organization. Constituencies is a more encompassing term, used to refer to any stakeholder group or organization that is important to the work of a program, department or organization—either because it benefits from, influences or is influenced by the organization. Thus, advisory or regulatory boards, other departments that provide resources, departments with which you collaborate or the senior administration might not be beneficiaries of the work of your organization in the most precise sense of the term, but they would certainly be important constituencies.

[22] This may include potential customers who chose the products, programs or services of a competitor, or an employee who was unaware of an employee benefit. It might also include employees who chose not to apply for open positions within the organization or rejected positions that were offered, potential sponsors who chose to fund other programs or projects, or potential collaborators or partnering groups who chose other organizations or options.

3.2 RELATIONSHIP ENHANCEMENT

1. How is information about beneficiary and constituent group needs, expectations, experiences, perspectives and satisfaction levels used to improve organizational procedures and practices and to enhance relationships?

   ▸ How is information on needs and expectations shared?

   ▸ How is that information used to guide planning and organizational improvement?

   ▸ How is the impact of improvements monitored and assessed?

2. How do the organizations determine the information and communication needs of groups and organizations for which products, programs and services are provided?

3. How are customers, employees, other important constituent groups and the general public appropriately informed about the program, department or organization?

4. How is basic information about your products, programs or services conveyed to potential and current beneficiaries?[23]

   ▸ How are web-based and other technologies used to simplify access to and use of information and services?

   ▸ How does the organization ensure that people have access to information about particular products, programs and services at times and places that are convenient and appropriate to their needs?

5. What are the various face-to-face situations[24] through which regular contact occurs between your communication organization and members of your beneficiary or constituency groups?

   ▸ What individuals and groups from your organization have regular and significant contact with members of your beneficiary and constituency groups?

   ▸ How does your organization monitor the quality of initial contact and ongoing interactions with those groups to ensure that courtesy, responsiveness, professionalism, and other values and standards are upheld?

6. What channels are available for people who are seeking special assistance or who want to make suggestions or register complaints? How does the organization ensure prompt and effective follow-up on complaints, suggestions or other types of feedback?

7. How does the organization monitor its effectiveness in addressing the information and communication needs and expectations of beneficiary and constituency groups?

---

[23] In the case of recipients of non-profit services, for example, how do you inform eligible recipients about where to find information about deadlines, services, resources and support, and where and how inquiries on various topics can be made?

[24] Examples might include interaction with employees during "walk-in" hours or scheduled appointments in a public service office.

CHAPTER 7 / Products, Programs, Services and Associated Processes 4.0

Communication organizations give life to their mission, aspirations and values through their products, programs, services and associated processes. Through these initiatives, the expertise of employees and the other resources of the organization are made available to customers, other beneficiary and constituency groups, and society at large.

Core Communication focuses on units in which communication is the core business. The core communication functions may involve community relations, corporate communication, investor relations, marketing, MARCOM (marketing/communication), media relations or public relations. These various departments or functions can be found within a centralized communication division or reporting to a variety of different areas, such as: development, finance, information services, human resources, marketing and strategy, to name a few possibilities.

Many other organizations certainly engage in communication, but their work is not fundamentally involved in the creation and dissemination of communication products, programs, services and their associated processes. Examples are units such as sales, human resources or computing services, each of which has multiple communication-related functions. But for these organizations, communication is a support, rather than the core, activity.

Category 4 focuses on the way in which communication organizations design, support, standardize, implement, evaluate and improve their products, programs, services and associated processes to ensure quality. This process begins with a review of the mission and vision of the department or organization, and then asks whether existing products, programs, services and associated processes appropriately reflect those purposes, aspirations and directions. Are the products, programs, services and associated processes of high quality, responsive to beneficiary and constituent needs and expectations, and to the unique opportunities and challenges that present themselves given the overall organization's history, mission, vision, and other characteristics and considerations?

MISSION-CRITICAL COMMUNICATION PRODUCTS, PROGRAMS, SERVICES AND ASSOCIATED PROCESSES / For communication organizations, the mission-critical products, programs, services and associated processes are those that are directly associated with aiding the organization in accomplishing its mission (Potter, 1999). The nature of what would be considered core products, programs or services varies depending on the kind of communication organization that is involved. For example, in a communication consulting firm, client prospecting, audience research and vendor relations would be examples of mission-critical programs. For internally-focused communication professionals, the following would serve as examples of mission-critical programs:

▸ Strategic planning.

▸ Developing and implementing communication plans.

▸ Building relationships between organizational sites and departments.

▸ Communication between organizational sites.

▸ Managing day-to-day communication.

▸ Communicating the organizational strategic plan.

▸ Managing employee programs, such as the employee newsletter, benefits information, etc.

Externally-focused communication functions would include:

▸ Strategic planning.

▸ Developing and implementing communication plans.

▸ Executing communication strategy to stakeholders.

▸ Developing communications to stakeholders and users.

▸ Creating presentations and sales aids.

▸ Developing and executing media relations programs.

▸ Building, maintaining and evolving relationships with the media (both news and trade).

▸ Scriptwriting, training and coaching for executives and spokespeople.

▸ Drafting press releases.

▸ Developing and maintaining a speakers bureau.

▸ Coordinating seminars, retreats and conferences.

▸ PR.

▶ MARCOM.

▶ Branding.

▶ Managing and updating the web site.

▶ Developing communication materials such as brochures, annual reports, newsletters, catalogs, etc.

OPERATIONAL AND SUPPORT SERVICES / For the organization as a whole, as well as for the numerous departments that compose it, there are also a number of behind-the-scenes operational activities that provide the infrastructure necessary to support the core communication functions. Often, these kinds of products, programs, services and associated processes are invisible to external groups. For example, support processes for the communication organization might include budgeting, facilities management, vendor relations, equipment procurement and maintenance, and hiring and training of employees.

PROCESSES / Whether one thinks of mission-critical or support activities, the devil is often in the details. That is to say, the overall quality of any product, program or service is largely a by-product of the effectiveness and efficiency of a number of detailed sequences of activities—or *processes*—and how these come together. Figure 6 illustrates these relationships.

FIGURE 6. PRODUCTS, PROGRAMS, SERVICES AND PROCESSES

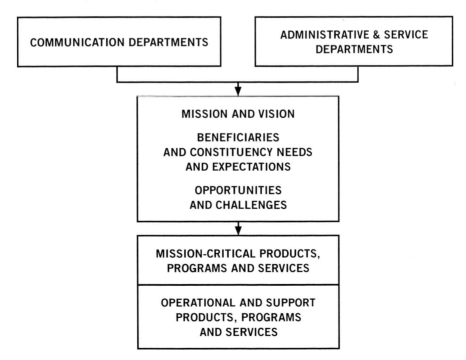

_49

To be most useful, a review should broadly focus on products, programs and services but also more closely examine the key processes that go into making a product, program or service. In the case of communication-related products, programs and services, for example, one can identify and examine a number of processes that are important to new products, employees and service/outreach, a sampling of which are listed in Figure 7.

FIGURE 7. COMMUNICATION PRODUCTS, PROGRAMS AND SERVICES, AND EXAMPLES OF ASSOCIATED PROCESSES

Product/Program/Service: New Product Development Associated Processes

▸ Understanding end user needs.

▸ Developing new products.

▸ Marketing new products.

▸ Delivering new products.

▸ Servicing new products.

▸ Defining new product goals.

▸ Evaluating goals/outcomes/effectiveness of product.

▸ Communicating new product information to internal and external beneficiaries and constituencies.

▸ Developing opportunities for end user feedback and participation.

▸ Advancing the use of employee expertise.

▸ Facilitating interdepartmental and/or interorganizational collaboration.

Product/Program/Service: Employee Communication Associated Processes

▸ Understanding employee needs.

▸ Communicating relevant organizational information to employees when and where they need it.

▸ Developing opportunities for employee feedback and participation.

▸ Facilitating interdepartmental and/or interorganizational collaboration.

▸ Advancing the use of employee expertise.

▸ Evaluating the goals/outcomes/effectiveness of the program or service.

Product/Program/Service: Outreach and Public Service Associated Processes

▸ Understanding end user needs.

▸ Developing community outreach initiatives (prospective customers, legislators, corporate partners) and communicating with them.

▸ Advancing the use of employee expertise.

▸ Promoting volunteerism.

▸ Partnering with other sectors and organizations.

▸ Facilitating interdepartmental and/or interorganizational collaboration.

▸ Developing opportunities for end user feedback and participation.

▸ Evaluating the goals/outcomes/effectiveness of the program or service.

The focus of a review is to determine the quality and effectiveness of communication products, programs and services overall, focusing also on the extent to which associated processes are thoughtfully designed, appropriately supported, sufficiently standardized and documented, efficiently implemented, periodically evaluated, and regularly improved, as well as whether they meet constituent needs and expectations. The careful review of processes to be sure that they "add value" has long been an important criterion for Baldrige-based assessment (Baldrige, 2006).

The same kind of analysis can be applied to a review of operational and support activities and their associated processes, as illustrated in Figure 8.

FIGURE 8. OPERATIONAL AND SUPPORT SERVICES AND EXAMPLES OF ASSOCIATED PROCESSES
Operational/Support Activity Associated Processes

▸ Budgeting and managing financial processes.

▸ Developing and overseeing contractual arrangements (government, industry, other organizations).

▸ Coordinating resources (financial, building, fiscal).

▸ Allocating and evaluating space and resources.

▸ Ordering equipment.

▸ Developing and overseeing procedures for maintaining records (reliability, confidentiality, accessibility, security).

> ‣ Managing computer technology and applications.
>
> ‣ Managing vendor relationships.

PROCESS ANALYSIS / A review of products, programs and services involves identifying and analyzing mission-critical products, programs, and services and their associated processes. It also includes an analysis of important operational and support services, and the processes associated with those areas. But how does one analyze a process? For illustrative purposes, consider a nonprofit organization with the goal of serving its constituents. In this example, a number of associated processes can be examined, including the process involved in developing a new service.

To analyze the effectiveness and efficiency of processes, it is helpful to develop flowcharts that identify and describe the various steps involved. Figure 9 provides an example of a flowchart of the steps involved in developing a new service. Dissecting a process in this way helps to clarify the details of the process, determine how well it works, and potentially improve its effectiveness and efficiency. In this case, the process analysis reveals why it takes so long to offer a new service. As it presently operates, the process may well meet organizational needs for quality and/or protocol; however, if it takes many months to achieve that goal because of the complexity involved, the needs and expectations of the constituencies are not being met. Systematic study can help determine whether steps can be shortened or eliminated, procedures streamlined, additional training provided to improve efficiency, technology introduced to expedite the process, and so on. An analysis of this kind generally results in improved processes—processes that are more efficient, more effective and more responsive to the needs of all parties involved. This approach also results in documented, standardized key processes that can be easily communicated, understood and replicated.

FIGURE 9. SAMPLE FLOWCHART: THE PROCESS FOR DEVELOPING A NEW SERVICE

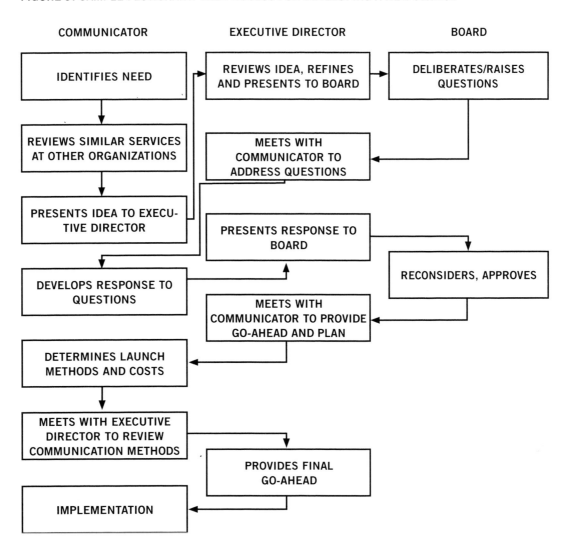

INTERDEPARTMENTAL AND CROSS-FUNCTIONAL PROCESSES / In some cases, mission-critical processes require collaboration with external groups and organizations. Such processes may take place in alliances, partnerships and supplier relations between organizations or between departments within an organization. Examples include web site development and materials/publications for products, programs, materials, resources or services.

COMPARISONS / Drawing comparisons between processes in one's products, programs and services and others internal and external to the organization is important for work analysis and improvement. Opportunities also need to be created to analyze and learn from peers, competitors and leaders in one's area, and where appropriate, from organizations in other sectors/markets. Through this kind of activity, more effective mission-critical, support and operational processes can be identified, studied and adopted.

4.0 PRODUCTS, PROGRAMS, SERVICES AND ASSOCIATED PROCESSES: KEY REVIEW ISSUES

Category 4 focuses on the products, programs, and services—and their associated processes—that are essential to accomplishing and advancing your mission. Also considered are important support and operational activities and their processes. In each case, the focus is on how the products, programs and services—and associated processes—are designed, supported, standardized, implemented, evaluated and improved.

4.1 MISSION-CRITICAL PRODUCTS, PROGRAMS, SERVICES AND ASSOCIATED PROCESSES

1. What are the mission-critical products, programs and services—and the most important associated processes—of the organization?

    ▸ How is each product, program or service related to the mission, vision and broad organizational goals?

    ▸ What beneficiary and constituency groups[25] are served by specific products, programs and services?

    ▸ What are the specific goals and intended outcomes of each product, program or service?[26]

    ▸ For each product, program or service area, what are the most critical associated processes?[27]

---

[25] Beneficiary and constituency groups refers broadly to individuals, groups or organizations—variously termed stakeholders, customers, audiences, users, consumers, clients or publics—for whom you provide products, programs or services, who benefit directly or indirectly from your work, or who have an important influence on your organization's success. The list of such groups will, of course, depend on the mission of the organization and will be different for profit and nonprofit organizations. Profit groups might include shareholders, customers, vendors, consultants, professional associations, advisory boards, bargaining units, local and state government, the citizens of the community or state, the mass media, and others. In addition to those for-profit groups, nonprofit groups might include volunteers, the public, visitors, families of those that are served, guiding councils, colleges and universities, and many more. Note: Employees are a critical constituency group for all programs, departments and organizations. They are the focus of Category 5 and, therefore, are not considered in this category.

[26] Identification of specific goals and intended outcomes would include clarifying product and program expectations and outcomes, as well as focusing on specifying the particular aims and purposes of services provided.

[27] Processes refers to the sequences of work activities that are associated with fulfillment of an organization's, department's or program's mission and its activities, products, programs and services. Processes associated with mission-critical products, programs and services are those for which the organization has a particular expertise. For communication organizations, mission-critical

2. What approaches are used to achieve and maintain high standards in each mission-critical product, program and service, and in the associated processes? More specifically, for products, programs, and services and their associated processes, how are high standards achieved in:

   ▸ *Designing* new product, program or service offerings?

   ▸ *Supporting* products, programs and services with appropriate fiscal, technical, human and physical resources?

   ▸ *Standardizing* and *documenting* processes and procedures to ensure an appropriate level of reliability and consistency?

   ▸ *Implementing* products, programs and services and their associated processes?

   ▸ *Evaluating* product, program, service and process outcomes?

   ▸ *Improving* current offerings and *identifying* possibilities for new or refined products, programs and services based on the results?

3. How do you determine the quality and effectiveness of product, program and service offerings, and of their associated processes, and how is this information used for monitoring and improvement?

   ▸ How do you determine if products, programs and services are achieving their goals and results?[28]

   ▸ How are the assessment results used to provide feedback, as appropriate, to customers, employees, and other relevant beneficiaries and constituencies?

   ▸ How are assessments used to guide reviews and improvement of product, program and service offerings?

4. How does the organization ensure that new and existing communication products, programs and services, and their associated processes, benefit from the latest and most appropriate technological innovation?

5. What groups or organizations play a critical role as partners or collaborators with mission-critical processes, and how are high standards of quality established and maintained in collaborative work with those organizations?

---

work processes typically include activities directly associated with the understanding of information, communication and awareness. Other organizations' mission-critical processes will vary greatly depending on their mission, vision and goals.

[28] Determining the quality, effectiveness or success of products, programs or services requires the development of evaluative criteria in terms of which such judgments can be made. Evaluative criteria can take on the shape of intended goals and results, which might include: results from clients with repeat and referral business or results from audiences with product recognition, sales, service awareness/knowledge, comprehension/understanding, etc. The topic of assessment is discussed more fully in Category 6.

6. How are peer, competitor and leading communication organizations selected for purposes of comparative assessment with your communication products, programs, services and associated processes? How is the information gained from comparisons used in monitoring, measurement and improvement?

7. How often are mission-critical products, programs, services and associated processes reviewed and refined?

4.2 OPERATIONAL AND SUPPORT SERVICES AND PROCESSES

1. What are your key operational and support services—and their associated processes?

   ▸ How is each necessary to support mission-critical products, programs and services?

   ▸ For each operational and support service, what are the most critical processes?[29]

2. How do you determine if your operational and support services and their associated processes—including budgeting and finance—are effective and efficient, and how is this information used for improving these services?

3. What approaches are used to achieve and maintain high standards in each operational and support service, and in the associated processes? More specifically, how are high standards achieved in:

   ▸ *Designing* new support services?

   ▸ *Supporting* these services with appropriate fiscal, technical, human and physical resources?

   ▸ *Standardizing* and *documenting* processes and procedures to ensure an appropriate level of reliability and consistency of support processes?

   ▸ *Implementing* support services and their associated processes?

   ▸ *Evaluating* support service and results?

   ▸ *Improving* current services and *identifying* possibilities for new or refined support services based on the results?

---

[29] Operational, support services and processes are necessary to assist in the fulfillment of your mission and in the development and implementation of your products, programs and services. Often, such processes are invisible to external groups— for example, maintaining client and media lists, working with vendors such as printers and freelance writers and designers, preparing for meetings and client visits, data entry, mass mailings, brainstorming sessions, cultivating relationships with media (both trade and news) and vendors, managing staff, project management, photo management, archiving, research, design, fiscal management, budgeting, recruiting and hiring, conducting performance reviews, training, purchasing equipment and supplies, coordinating repairs and maintenance—especially IT-related—time and room scheduling, preparing work materials, scheduling and conducting meetings, and so on.

4. How does the organization ensure that new and existing operational and support services and their associated processes benefit from the latest and most appropriate technological innovations?

5. What groups or organizations play a critical role as partners, collaborators, or operational and support services and processes, and how do you ensure that high standards of quality are established and maintained in collaborative work with those organizations?

6. How are peer, competitor and leading organizations selected for purposes of comparative assessment of your operational and support services and their associated processes, and how is the information gained from comparisons used for improvement?

7. How often are your operational and support areas and processes reviewed and refined?

CHAPTER 8/Employee Satisfaction and Workplace Climate 5.0

Recruiting, developing and retaining outstanding employees is one of the most critical activities in any business. To a great extent, the people who work in communication organizations determine the quality of the products, programs, services and associated processes that can be offered. In addition, they lead the organization by increasing shared understanding between and among its constituents. Employees working on a specific project, for a certain work group or team, in a certain department and within an organization are all important sources of impressions of the product, program, service, department and the organization itself.

Because the organization's mission is so dependent on employees, creating a workplace with a positive culture and practices that encourage, recognize and reward effectiveness, innovation and professional development is a vital goal. It is important to create a climate that is engaging, personally and professionally satisfying, and supportive.

5.0 EMPLOYEE SATISFACTION AND WORKPLACE CLIMATE: KEY REVIEW ISSUES

This category focuses on factors that contribute to creating a superior workplace and an outstanding, well-trained, engaged, collaborative and committed employee base. Also considered are issues related to employee standards, orientation, review and recognition, learning and professional development, and satisfaction assessment. Consideration of workplace practices includes organizational structure, positions and responsibilities, and workplace environment and climate.

5.1 EMPLOYEES: AREAS TO ADDRESS

A. Standards and Orientation

1. What approaches are used to recruit, hire and retain employees?[30]

   ▸ How does the organization identify its employee needs?

   ▸ How are the necessary employee credentials and competencies determined?

   ▸ What methods are used for recruiting, hiring and retaining employees?

   ▸ How are standards and expectations for candidates for open positions established and communicated?

2. What kinds of orientation programs and/or mentoring experiences are provided for new employees? For what groups are these provided, and by whom?

---

[30] Employee is used to refer to all full- and part-time salaried, non-salaried and volunteer employee and non-employee groups.

3. How is basic job-related information provided relative to:

   ▶ Salary and benefits?

   ▶ Core competencies for jobs?

   ▶ Performance appraisals and reviews?

   ▶ Promotion review processes?

   ▶ The treatment of customers and/or colleagues?

   ▶ Ethics and integrity?

   ▶ Conflicts of interest?

   ▶ Diversity and discrimination?

   ▶ Privacy?

   ▶ Intellectual property?

   ▶ Affirmative action?

   ▶ Grievances and internal disputes?

   ▶ Required training and certifications?

B. Review and Recognition[31]

   1. How do performance review procedures ensure useful and timely feedback for employee groups?

   2. How are review and recognition systems and practices used to encourage, recognize and reward superior performance?

   3. How do compensation, benefits and related reward and incentive practices support and reinforce organizational directions and priorities?

   4. How are nonfinancial rewards, practices and/or events used to recognize individual and collective effectiveness, and to reinforce organizational directions and priorities?[32]

   5. How, and how often, does the organization assess and improve its performance review and recognition systems?

---

[31] Recognition includes, but is not limited to, public acknowledgment of individuals and groups/teams, personal feedback and merit awards. Also included are letters of commendation, certifications of merit, articles in bulletins or newsletters, announcements at meetings, and so forth.

[32] See note 30.

C. Learning and Professional Development

1. How does the communication organization identify new knowledge, skills and capabilities needed by current employees? How are each of the following taken into account:

   ▸ Directions, aspirations, priorities, goals and plans of the organization?

   ▸ The needs, capabilities and perspectives of employees?

   ▸ Job performance review outcomes?

   ▸ Requirements for certification, licensure or accreditation?

   ▸ Changing technology?

   ▸ Evolving institutional or marketplace needs and expectations?

2. What personal and professional learning and development[33] opportunities are provided for employee groups?

   ▸ How are participation and engagement in program, department, organization, and other development activities and events encouraged for each employee group?

   ▸ What leadership and skill development opportunities are provided?

   ▸ How is career development guidance provided?

3. What approaches are used to deliver professional education and development?[34]

4. How are professional education and development opportunities evaluated, and how are results used for improvement?

5. How are special education and training needs, such as leadership development, technology training, diversity awareness, trades training, etc., addressed? Who is responsible for providing the resources for such training, and how are these programs evaluated?

---

[33] This might include professional development programs, flextime before or after work to permit enrollment in professional development activities, funding for participation in professional association programs, and sabbaticals.

[34] Professional development might include orientations, traditional academic courses, computer-based instruction, distance education, on-site programs, off-site programs, consultants or self-paced instruction.

D. Employee Well-Being and Satisfaction

1. How does the organization learn about employee experiences, needs, expectations, and sources of satisfaction and dissatisfaction?[35]

2. How is information related to employee satisfaction used to enhance workplace satisfaction and morale?

    ▶ How is information on needs and expectations shared?

    ▶ How is this information used to guide planning and organizational improvement?

    ▶ How is the impact of improvements monitored?

3. How does the level of employee satisfaction in your organization compare with peer, competitor and/or other leaders, and how is that comparison information used?

4. How, and how often, does your organization review and refine your approaches to employee satisfaction assessment?

5.2 WORKPLACE AREAS TO ADDRESS

A. Structure

1. What is the organizational structure of the program, department and/or institution?

    ▶ What is the size of each of the major areas or work groups within the organization?

    ▶ What is the primary function of each?

2. How does the organization determine the appropriateness of particular organizational structures for:

    ▶ Advancing your mission and aspirations?

    ▶ Effectively utilizing employee capabilities?

    ▶ Managing resources and workloads equitably?

    ▶ Considering the needs and expectations of beneficiaries, constituencies and employees?

    ▶ Ensuring appropriate engagement opportunities for employees.

---

[35] These factors might be assessed through surveys or interviews, retention rates, absenteeism, grievance rates, analysis of exit interviews, or other indicators established by the organization. Further discussion of assessment, comparisons and outcomes is provided in Categories 6 and 7.

> ▸ Aligning with national standards for functional operations (e.g., IABC and SHRM)?[36]

> ▸ Ensuring proper controls to maintain operational integrity (e.g., financial, employee and information technology)?

3. How does your program, department or institution review and improve its organizational structure?

B. Positions and Responsibilities

1. How does the organization develop and communicate position descriptions, associated responsibilities and performance standards?

2. How does your organization design, organize and oversee work practices to encourage:

> ▸ Individual efficiency?

> ▸ Departmental and organizational efficiency?

> ▸ Collegiality?

> ▸ Collaboration?

> ▸ Innovation?

> ▸ Valuing diversity (including age, race, ethnicity and gender)?

> ▸ Appreciation of organizational and departmental ethical principles and values?

3. How is organizational flexibility encouraged? For instance, how are the following used:

> ▸ Cross-training?

> ▸ Redesign of work processes?

> ▸ Job rotation?

> ▸ Technology?

> ▸ Simplification and reduction of job classification?

C. Workplace Environment and Culture

1. What approaches are used by the program, department and/or institution to maintain a healthy, safe and secure work environment?

---

[36] See the International Association for Business Communicators (http://www.iabc.com) and the Society for Human Resource Management (http://www.shrm.com).

2. How does the organization identify improvement needs and monitor progress in the areas of health, safety and security?

3. What approaches are used to ensure that appropriate health and safety standards and/or regulatory requirements are maintained relative to the organization's:

   ▶ Human resources?

   ▶ Physical resources?

   ▶ Equipment?

   ▶ Electronic and print services and products?

   ▶ Photography studios?

   ▶ Focus group studios?

   ▶ Computers?

4. How does the organization prepare for emergencies or disasters—such as preparedness for natural disasters, disaster recovery plans for information technology systems, continuity planning or plans for dealing with employee emergencies.

5. What approaches are used to create a positive and congenial workplace climate?

6. How does the organization promote and reward collegiality, collaboration and teamwork among employee groups?

7. How does the organization assess workplace climate, and how is this information used for improvement?

8. How, and how often, are approaches to workplace climate assessment reviewed and refined?

CHAPTER 9 / Assessment and Information Use 6.0

As discussed in the previous sections, attention to leadership; strategic planning; beneficiaries and constituencies; products, programs, services and processes; and employee satisfaction and workplace climate are essential to organizational effectiveness. This category focuses on how progress, achievements and outcomes are assessed in each of those areas and, more generally, how you can assess the overall success of your organization in fulfilling its mission, aspirations and broad goals. This category also examines how you determine which peer, competitive or leading communication programs, departments or organizations to use for comparative assessment of your outcomes, and how to make use of this information. Finally, this category focuses on how the knowledge gained from assessment, and the expertise and experience of employees, is shared and used to improve the effectiveness of your organization and its products, programs, services and associated processes.

INCREASING ATTENTION TO ASSESSMENT / "The communicator, like any other business manager, must think, act, and manage communication programs strategically, recording measurable results that help accomplish the organization's mission" (Potter, 1999, p. 12). Not surprisingly, the topic of assessment has received increasing attention in recent years in both communication and other organizations. Most often, discussions are linked to calls for increased accountability and performance measurement. As expectations increase and resources remain constant or decrease, evaluations of how well a particular communication organization is succeeding in its work, the extent of return on investment and, more specifically, what is working well and what isn't, become essential for planning and resource allocation (Brancato, 1995; Kaplan & Norton, 1996, 2001; Ruben, 2004).

Assessment, outcomes measurement and evidence have long been fundamental themes of the Baldrige framework. The emphasis of this category is on the methods in which the communication organization uses research-based plans and assessment to review products, programs and services to provide continuous results towards aiding the organization as a whole in meeting its goals and mission (Potter, 1999; Sinickas, 1999).

For employees and other constituencies, products, programs, services and desired outcomes will vary substantially from department to department, reflecting each department's particular mission. In each case, however, the assessment of the effectiveness of products, programs and services presuppose that goals are well established. Clear goals help to promote effective communication with beneficiaries and constituencies, foster better alignment of expectations among all parties, and provide the necessary foundation for assessment.

At a macro level, assessment focuses broadly on an entire program or department or on organizational purposes, aspirations and goals. Typical measures at this level of analysis include customer retention and reorder rates, organizational profit, market share, growth figures, pertinent rankings and other high-level indicators of organizational effectiveness. At a more micro level, assessment within departmental units considers the quality and effectiveness of specific product, program and service offerings—such as the profitability of a specific product or service, the satisfaction level of clients, or the number of employees aware of and using specific employee benefits.

Beyond its importance for the purposes of accountability, there are a number of far-reaching benefits for the organization when a program of assessment is thoughtfully planned and executed (Kaplan & Norton, 1996, 2001; Ruben 2004). They include the following:

- Stimulating dialogue and clarifying the organization's mission, aspirations and priorities.

- Heightening the shared sense of the purposes of products, programs and services.

- Developing a shared perspective on the appropriate standards and indicators of effectiveness.

- Identifying current strengths.

- Clarifying improvement needs.

- Providing meaningful comparisons.

- Heightening personal and collective responsibility.

- Encouraging, monitoring and documenting progress.

- Providing a foundation for fact-based planning, decision making and problem solving.

- Energizing and motivating employees.

- Providing the basis for more effective communication about program, department or organizational strengths.

Each of these benefits is achievable if the assessment planning and implementation process is undertaken in a way that appropriately engages members of the organization in determining what to measure and why, and how to use results.

STEPS IN THE ASSESSMENT PROCESS / Typically, the assessment process begins with defining (or reviewing) the organization's mission, vision and broad organizational goals. Some of these goals should relate to organizational effectiveness and to organizational functions associated with:

- ▶ Leadership.

- ▶ Strategic planning.

- ▶ Beneficiaries and constituencies.

- ▶ Products, programs, services and processes.

- ▶ Support and operational services and processes.

- ▶ Employees and workplace issues.

While not all of these areas map directly to the bottom line in the short run, their significance to the long-term well-being of the organization is clear (NIST, 2006).

In reviewing the statements of purpose and aspirations, the essential question is: How do we know if we are succeeding in our work? Or, more precisely: What kind of evidence do we need to determine whether we are successful in achieving our mission-critical goals and aspirations; in developing and delivering effective products, programs and services; and, more generally, in creating an effective department and/or organization? The challenge, then, is to decide what information and evidence would be needed to make these determinations, how to gather this information, what useful data may already be available, and ultimately, how to integrate and use the resulting information and evidence to drive improvement.

Regardless of whether the assessment process will be for an entire communication organization or a specific department or program, the objective is to effectively integrate the assessment process into the life of the organization. The specifics and language will, of course, vary somewhat depending on the nature of the unit involved. Broadly stated, here are the steps:

1. Clarify purposes, aspirations and broad organizational goals.

2. Assess outcomes and achievements relative to purposes; aspirations and goals; products, programs and services; and other factors that are necessary for organizational effectiveness. This should include comparisons of outcomes over time, and with peers and other organizations.

3. Monitor and use results for documenting outcomes and achievements; informing day-to-day decision making and resource allocation; improving product, program and service offerings and their associated processes; and generally enhancing quality and effectiveness.

Figure 10 provides a more detailed template for the steps involved in establishing an integrated assessment framework.[37]

FIGURE 10. STEPS TO DEVELOP AN INTEGRATED ASSESSMENT PROCESS

1. Define or Clarify Goals

    ▸ Identify and consider the needs and expectations of beneficiaries and constituencies and other key factors.

    ▸ Establish clear and shared goals for product, program, and service areas and offerings.

    ▸ Be certain that goals cover the full range of relevant activities.

    ▸ Clearly communicate goals to beneficiaries and constituencies.

2. Evaluate Outcomes

    ▸ Use established goals to guide assessment activities at all levels in your organization.

    ▸ Develop and use appropriate outcomes indicators, criteria, measures and evaluative procedures.

    ▸ Assess the extent to which established goals are being met within product, program and service areas as well as their associated processes, and more generally, identify gaps.

    ▸ Make comparisons with peers and other institutions.

    ▸ Confirm that assessment covers all defined goals and other factors associated with organizational effectiveness.

3. Use the Outcomes Information

    ▸ Communicate the results of assessment to colleagues within the organization and to beneficiary and constituency groups, as appropriate.

    ▸ Compare outcomes information, as appropriate, with results from previous years and with those from peer, competitor and/or leading organizations to identify patterns and trends.

---

[37] The authors gratefully acknowledge the influence of the Middle States Commission on Higher Education (MSCHE) publications (2002, 2003a, 2003b) and discussions with Jean Avnet Morse, MSCHE President, in the development of this general model of assessment planning.

> ▶ Use outcomes information to improve products, programs, services and associated processes and, generally, the effectiveness of the program, department or organization.
>
> ▶ Integrate outcomes information into formal and informal planning and decision making activities.
>
> ▶ Periodically review and, as appropriate, refine and update your goals, assessment procedures and approaches to using this information.

ESTABLISHING INDICATORS / Step 1 focuses on defining goals. That topic was discussed under Category 2, Strategic Planning, and also, more briefly, under Category 4, Products, Programs, Services and Associated Processes. Clear, shared goals provide a necessary foundation for assessing outcomes.

Step 2 calls for the selection of criteria that make it possible to monitor progress and assess outcomes. The establishment of such indicators involves the translation of broad, organizational goals into standards that can be measured. For instance, if one departmental goal is to "recruit and retain experienced employees," you will need indicators that capture the level of experience of employees applying for positions, and secondarily, whether those people were retained. *Level of experience* might be measured by number of years in relevant positions prior to applying to the position, and number of years of continued employment would be one simple measure of retention.

ASSESSMENT IN ADMINISTRATIVE AND SERVICE DEPARTMENTS / For administrative and service departments, a number of indicators and measures are available. The choice as to which to select and measure depends on the department's purposes, aspirations, broad organizational goals, and specific products, programs and services. The listing in Figure 11 provides a sampling of possible indicators.

FIGURE 11. POTENTIAL ASSESSMENT INDICATORS FOR ADMINISTRATIVE AND SERVICE DEPARTMENTS

Mission-Critical Products, Programs, Services and Associated Processes

- Effectiveness
- Efficiency
- Reliability
- Cycle time
- Resource utilization
- Increased collaboration among participants

Beneficiary and Constituency Relations

- Effectiveness and efficiency of assessment approach.
- Comprehension and understanding of key communication initiatives.
- Satisfaction with products, programs, services and associated processes.
- Positive and improving reputation for quality and service.
- Positive behavior change related to key communication initiatives.
- Positive relationships with vendors, such as consultants, printers, photographers, web designers, etc.

Employee and Workplace Satisfaction

- Recruitment
- Attractiveness
- Turnover/retention
- Compensation
- Organizational culture and climate
- Morale
- Perks

Operational and Support Services

▶ Financial mangement effectiveness.

▶ Staff recruiting and training effectiveness.

▶ Adequacy of technology.

▶ Effectiveness and efficiency of equipment and facilities management.

Professional Development

▶ Courses/programs offered

▶ Participation

▶ Satisfaction

▶ Staff needs addressed

▶ Learning outcomes

▶ Adequacy of support

▶ Impact on service and advancement

▶ Monetary support

ASSESSMENT IN COMMUNICATION PROGRAMS, DEPARTMENTS AND ORGANIZA-TIONS / For communication programs, the general steps presented in Figure 10 would include an emphasis on issues of behavioral change outcomes in employee communication programs as illustrated in Figure 12. The establishment of indicators involves the use of specific, measurable statements and the actions/tactics that support the organizational goals, with assessment measures built in—either by means of qualitative or quantitative analysis (Hettinger & Hattori, 2006; Sinickas, 1999).

FIGURE 12. ASSESSING BEHAVIORAL CHANGE OUTCOMES IN EMPLOYEE COMMUNICATION PROGRAMS

1. Define Behavioral Change Goals

    ▸ Consider employee needs and expectations, as well as key issues.

    ▸ Establish clear and shared goals for specific programs, services, professional development programs and stages (e.g., different health care plans and levels to match different employee age groups).

    ▸ Confirm that behavioral change goals cover the full range of relevant activities, including health care, the employee assistance program, general organizational information, retirement plan information, etc.

    ▸ Communicate the goals to employees and other appropriate constituency groups.

2. Evaluate Behavioral Change Outcomes

    ▸ Develop appropriate behavioral change outcomes indicators, measures and measurement procedures.

    ▸ Confirm that specific activities within the organization cover all of the defined goals at increasing levels of difficulty and with effective coordination across the organization (e.g., assurance of appropriate coherence and avoidance of unnecessary duplication).

    ▸ Assess the extent to which established goals are being met with specific programs, services, professional development programs and their associated processes.

3. Use the Outcomes Information

    ▸ Communicate the results to employees and, as appropriate, to external constituents.

    ▸ Use outcomes information to improve all programs at all levels.

    ▸ Compare outcomes, as appropriate, with results from previous years and with those from peer, competitor and/or leading organizations.

    ▸ Integrate results from behavioral change assessment with overall organizational assessment.

    ▸ Use the results to guide planning, resource allocation and day-to-day decision making.

    ▸ Periodically review and, as appropriate, refine and update goals and the effectiveness of the processes involved in defining behavioral change goals, evaluating outcomes and using evaluative information for improvement.

For instance, if the behavioral change goals of an employee program include increasing the percentage of employees participating in a higher-end health care plan, involving employees in the rollout process, and encouraging them to engage other employees in signing up for the new health care plan, then the task assessment challenge is to identify appropriate ways to measure the extent to which these goals are being realized. A number of potential indicators may be used to assess the three mission-critical areas, as illustrated in Figure 13.

FIGURE 13. POTENTIAL ASSESSMENT INDICATORS FOR COMMUNICATION PRODUCTS, PROGRAMS, DEPARTMENTS AND ORGANIZATIONS

BEHAVIORAL CHANGE
Program Quality Indicators

- ▶ Mission clarity.

- ▶ Documented behavioral change goals for all employee programs/services, consumer purchasing or service usage, repeat and referral business from clients.

- ▶ Comprehension and understanding of communication initiative.

- ▶ Expressed need for programs and offerings.

- ▶ Coherence across delivery to all operational and support services.

- ▶ Effective financial management.

- ▶ Effective staff recruiting and training.

- ▶ Adequacy of technology.

- ▶ Effectiveness and efficiency of equipment and facilities management users.

- ▶ Rigor.

- ▶ Communicator qualifications.

- ▶ Currency/comprehensiveness of product/program/service/process.

- ▶ Adequacy of support services.

- ▶ Organizational climate.

Employee/Consumer/Client Outcomes and Perception Indicators

- ▶ Behavioral change outcomes compared with program goals.

- Preference patterns of employees/consumers/clients.

- Selectivity level.

- Engagement opportunities.

- Expressed satisfaction levels.

- Retention rates.

- Interaction with communicator or program facilitator.

- Employee/consumer/client involvement with program rollout.

- Repeat users.

- Referrals from current users.

PUBLIC SERVICE/OUTREACH INDICATORS

Activity Levels and Contacts

- Invitations to speak at community and professional association events.

- Selection for leadership roles in the community and within professional associations.

- Expressed satisfaction levels.

- Peer assessments and review of credentials, accomplishments and records.

- Number and location of press release placements.

- Amount of media coverage.

KEY REFERENCE CONSTITUENCY GROUPS

- Prospective customers/clients

- Current customers/clients

- Prospective employees

- Current employees

- Organization and/or parent organization

- Profession/discipline

- Media (news and trade)

- ▸ Research agencies

- ▸ Regulatory agencies

- ▸ Families of employees

- ▸ Citizens

- ▸ Other employers

- ▸ Community

- ▸ Governing boards

- ▸ Accrediting boards and agencies

- ▸ Shareholders/investors

- ▸ Public at large

DASHBOARDS

Some programs, departments and organizations take the step of identifying a small set of key indicators and measures—sometimes termed *dashboard indicators*—that they use to track outcomes and monitor progress in the most critical areas, as illustrated in Figure 14. Dashboard indicators can be helpful in the same way that the gauges of an automobile's dashboard provide a quick reference to information on a vehicle's most important functions. Is the organization:

- ▸ Achieving its mission?

- ▸ Advancing its vision?

- ▸ Providing high-quality products, programs and services?

- ▸ Making progress on broad organization goals?

- ▸ Recruiting and retaining outstanding employees?

- ▸ Creating a positive workplace climate?

- ▸ Effectively addressing the needs of constituency groups for which products, programs and services are provided?

The information contained in the dashboard should provide effective communicators with a quick indicator as to how their program, department or organization as a whole is doing. At the same time, it is important to remember that these figures need to be based on accurate and reliable information.

FIGURE 14. SAMPLE DASHBOARD FOR AN EMPLOYEE COMMUNICATION DEPARTMENT

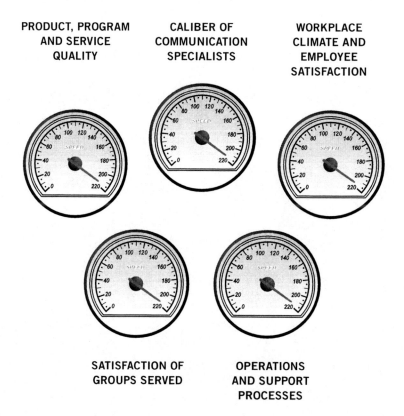

COMPARISONS / As noted earlier, comparing outcomes and achievements over time to identify trends and patterns, and to monitor progress, is an important component of assessment. Another useful type of comparison is with peers, leaders and, where appropriate, competitor organizations. Comparative assessment—also termed *benchmarking*—involves identifying, selecting and systematically gathering information from other organizations to compare your organization's performance with theirs. The most obvious sources of comparison are other communication programs, departments or organizations. For example, professional associations, such as IABC, often provide comparison information about the structure of communication organizations as well as in-depth reviews of specific communication programs. In some instances, it is helpful—or even necessary—to create benchmarking relationships with other organizations to get meaningful information for pertinent comparisons.

Depending on the nature of the communication organization, opportunities sometimes exist to draw comparisons with other industries that have similar processes or activities. For example, employee communication, facilities or purchasing processes may be compared with similar processes in organizations in other sectors. In all cases, comparisons are an important tool for placing one's current outcomes information in a broader context.

THE BROAD PURPOSES OF ASSESSMENT / Fundamentally, assessment is a means of monitoring the outcomes and achievements of a program, department or organization to determine how well it is succeeding in:

▸ Fulfilling its mission.

▸ Advancing its aspirations.

▸ Achieving its broad organizational goals.

▸ Creating and delivering high-quality products, programs and services.

▸ Addressing the needs and expectations of internal and external beneficiaries and constituencies.

▸ Functioning effectively and efficiently as an organization.

Assessment is a crucial part of any communication organization. It provides the information essential to understand how well your audience comprehends and acts upon your message. While the findings will sometimes be just what you expected, often they will surprise you (Sinickas, 1999). Of greater importance is the nature of the communicator's relationship with senior management—showing you can and do make a measurable impact on bottom-line business results will place the communicator at the top of the list to receive resources and recognition (Sinickas, 1999).

6.0 ASSESSMENT AND INFORMATION USE: KEY REVIEW ISSUES
This category focuses on how a communication organization conducts assessment and how the assessment process is integrated into the life of the organization so that information on progress, outcomes and achievements is used effectively to guide organizational planning, decision making and improvement efforts. Specifically, Category 6 asks about:

▸ Broad organizational goals and the indicators, evidence and measures associated with each.

▸ How evidence and measurement information is gathered and analyzed.

▸ How comparative information is shared and used to assess and improve products, programs, services and associated processes.

▶ The quality and effectiveness of the program, department and/or organization in general.

6.1 ASSESSMENT APPROACH AND METHODS: AREAS TO ADDRESS

A. Leadership Assessment

How does the communication organization assess the quality and effectiveness of its leadership and leadership practices? (See discussion in Category 1.)

▶ What indicators and measures[38] are used as the basis for assessment?

· ▶ How were those indicators and measures established?

▶ What information-gathering methods or procedures are employed?

▶ How are assessment results communicated to colleagues within the organization and, as appropriate, to beneficiary and constituency groups?

▶ How is outcomes information used to improve leadership practices and the organization in general?

▶ How does the organization periodically review and, as appropriate, refine and update assessment procedures and approaches to using this information?

B. Strategic Planning Assessment

How does the communication organization assess the quality and effectiveness of its strategic planning activities? (See the discussion in Category 2.)

▶ What indicators and measures[39] are used as the basis for assessment?

▶ How were those indicators and measures established?

---

[38] Various indicators, measures or other sources of evidence can be used for assessing outcomes, including trend data, survey data, comparisons, satisfaction indices, national norms or other outcomes, accreditation or review results, or focus group findings (Southern Association, 2003, p. 16).

In assessing the effectiveness of leadership and governance, evidence might include the implementation of new leadership feedback systems, improvements in leadership or leadership practices based on performance reviews or feedback, changes in organizational climate attributed to leadership initiatives, measures of leadership engagement, and service in leadership roles in external, public, or professional groups and organizations. See the discussion in Category 1.

[39] Various indicators, measures or other sources of evidence can be used for assessing the effectiveness of strategic planning, including the implementation of a new planning process, changes in the way goals and plans are established and measured, measures of employee engagement in the planning process, coordination of plans across departments or work groups, progress on goals, or the effectiveness of dissemination of information regarding plans. See the discussion in Category 2.

- What information-gathering methods or procedures are employed?

- How are assessment results communicated to colleagues within the organization and, as appropriate, to beneficiary and constituency groups?

- How is outcomes information used to improve strategic planning activities and the organization in general?

- How does the organization periodically review and, as appropriate, refine and update assessment procedures and approaches to using this information?

C. Beneficiaries and Constituencies Assessment

How does the organization assess the quality and effectiveness of its products, programs, departments, etc., in learning about beneficiary and constituency group needs, expectations and experiences, and in using the information to establish mutually satisfying relationships? (See the discussion in Category 3.)

- What indicators and measures[40] are used as the basis for assessment?

- How were those indicators and measures established?

- What information-gathering methods or procedures are employed?

- How are assessment results communicated to colleagues within the organization and, as appropriate, to other groups?

- How is outcomes information used to improve beneficiary and constituency group relationships and the organization in general?

- How does the organization periodically review and, as appropriate, refine and update assessment procedures and approaches to using this information?

[40] Indicators of the quality and effectiveness of relationships with beneficiary and constituency groups might include results from mail or phone surveys, focus groups, interviews, information from advisory groups, suggestion box responses, "mystery shoppers," and analysis of complaints and commendations. Also potentially useful, depending on the organization and the external groups involved, are indirect information-gathering methods such as the assessment of increased repeat and referral business, understanding and comprehension of key communication initiatives, positive behavior change related to key communication initiatives, increased collaboration, an increase in support from the parent organization as well as beneficiaries and constituencies, invitations and requests to serve in leadership roles in external groups, purchasing demand and trends, performance evaluations, complaint or suggestion content and rate, financial support, and many more. The appropriateness of methods will vary according to the organization, mission element and constituency group. Note: While it may be impossible to implement systematic assessment methods for all constituency groups, the presumption is that such methods should be in place for all priority beneficiary and constituency groups.

D. Products, Programs, Services and Associated Processes Assessment

1. Mission-Critical Products, Programs and Services, and Associated Processes

How does the organization assess the quality and effectiveness of its mission-critical communication products, programs and services, and their associated processes? (See the discussion in Category 4.1.)

> ‣ What indicators and measures[41] are used to assess mission-critical product, program and service offerings and their associated processes?

> ‣ How were those indicators and measures established?

> ‣ What information-gathering methods or procedures are employed?

> ‣ How are assessment results communicated to colleagues within the organization and, as appropriate, to other groups?

> ‣ How is outcomes information used to improve mission-critical products, programs, services and their associated processes, and the organization in general?

> ‣ How does the organization periodically review and, as appropriate, refine and update assessment procedures and approaches to using this information?

2. Operational and Support Services and Associated Processes

How does the organization assess the effectiveness and efficiency of important operational and support services and their associated processes? (See the discussion in Category 4.2.)

> ‣ What indicators and measures are used as the basis for assessment?

> ‣ How were those indicators and measures[42] established?

> ‣ What information-gathering methods or procedures are employed?

> ‣ How are assessment results communicated to colleagues within the organiza-

---

[41] For products, programs, services and associated processes, indicators might include product/program/service rankings (e.g., U.S. & World News ranking of hospitals in the U.S.), consumer/user retention rates, number of customers, number of new customers, time to market with new products/programs/services, profits, web site hits, etc. See discussion in Category 4.1.

[42] For operational and support services, indicators might include outcomes and achievements in areas that are largely invisible to external groups but essential to the effectiveness and efficiency of mission-critical products, programs and services and the functioning of the organization in general. Accomplishments that relate to the operational support of employee communication, for instance, would include scheduling, staffing, evaluation, purchasing, budgeting, employee recruitment and hiring, training and professional development, information management, e-mail and telephone systems, and logistical support of all types. Note: In some administrative organizations, the preceding processes listed as examples of organizational support activities may be mission-critical processes. For instance, in a human resources department, the work of a professional development office is likely to be regarded as mission critical. See the discussion in Category 4.2.

tion and, as appropriate, to other groups?

▸ How is outcomes information used to improve operational and support services, associated processes and the organization in general?

▸ How does the organization periodically review and, as appropriate, refine and update assessment procedures and approaches to using this information?

E. Employee Satisfaction and Workplace Climate Assessment

How does the organization assess its effectiveness in establishing a positive workplace, understanding and addressing employee needs, and evaluating employee satisfaction and workplace climate? (See the discussion in Category 5.)

▸ What indicators and measures are used as the basis for assessment?

▸ How were those indicators and measures[43] established?

▸ What information-gathering methods or procedures are employed?

▸ How are assessment results communicated to colleagues within the organization and, as appropriate, to other groups?

▸ How is outcomes information used to improve employee satisfaction, workplace climate and the organization in general?

▸ How does the organization periodically review and, as appropriate, refine and update assessment procedures and approaches to using this information?

F. Assessment and Information Use Assessment

How does the organization evaluate the effectiveness of its approaches to assessment and the sharing and use of information and expertise?

▸ What indicators and measures are used as the basis for assessment?

▸ How were those indicators and measures[44] established?

▸ What information-gathering methods or procedures are employed?

▸ How are assessment results communicated to colleagues within the organization

[43] Indicators of employee satisfaction and workplace climate might include the results of satisfaction or climate surveys or interviews, retention or turnover rates, absenteeism, analysis of exit interviews, or other indicators selected by the unit. See the discussion in Category 5.

[44] Evidence of outcomes and achievements in the area of assessment and information sharing might include improvements in performance measurement methods, advances in approaches to gathering and using comparison information from other organizations, measures of the effectiveness and/or efficiency of information dissemination and use, dissemination and adoption of "best practices," or improvements in information and information systems access, reliability, effectiveness or security. See the discussion in Category 6.

and, as appropriate, to other groups?

▸ How is outcomes information used to improve assessment and information sharing practices and the organization in general?

▸ How does the organization periodically review and, as appropriate, refine and update assessment procedures and approaches to using this information?

6.2 COMPARATIVE ANALYSIS[45]

1. How does the communication organization compare current outcomes information with results from previous years to identify themes and trends?

2. How does the organization use comparisons with peer, competitor and/or leading organizations to provide a context for interpreting outcomes and achievements?

3. How does the organization decide which peer, competitor or leading organizations to use for comparative analysis?

4. How does the organization keep its methods for gathering comparison information current with its needs and directions?

6.3 INFORMATION SHARING AND USE: AREAS TO ADDRESS

A. Availability and Dissemination

1. How does your organization ensure that data and information are collected, stored, retrieved and disseminated to ensure availability and access by appropriate individuals and departments?

2. What organizational information, including assessment results, is regularly communicated to internal and external groups? When and how does this take place?

▸ How does the organization determine which data and information to collect, store and disseminate?

▸ How do you ensure that your information systems are user-friendly?

▸ How does the organization keep software and hardware systems current with product, program and service needs and directions?

▸ How are the integrity, reliability, accuracy, timeliness, and security of data and

---

[45] Comparative analysis—also termed benchmarking—refers to the process of identifying, selecting and systematically gathering information from other organizations to compare your organization's performance, products, programs, services, processes, activities, achievements and/or impact with those of other organizations. Comparisons may be with peer and/or competitor organizations in other industries that have processes or activities comparable to yours. For example, facilities or purchasing processes may be compared with similar processes at peer or competitor organizations in other sectors. Comparisons with recognized leaders in business, health care, government or higher education organizations can provide a basis for setting goals for your own organization.

information ensured?

3. How does your organization address information and information technology policy issues, including:

- ▶ Access?

- ▶ Privacy and confidentiality?

- ▶ Internet use?

- ▶ Proprietary rights?

- ▶ Security?

B. Information and Knowledge Utilization

1. How does the organization encourage and reward the sharing and use of knowledge resources and expertise among individuals and departments within your organization?

2. How does the organization ensure that information reaches appropriate individuals, groups and organizations?

3. How does the organization determine whether the available forms and formats of data and information are appropriate and effective for addressing user needs, that they are adopted and that they are used?

CHAPTER 10/Outcomes and Achievements 7.0

For any communication organization, effectiveness and excellence are the ultimate aims. These purposes necessitate achieving and sustaining high standards relative to:

- ▶ Leadership
- ▶ Strategic planning
- ▶ Beneficiary and constituency relationships
- ▶ Products, programs, services and associated processes
- ▶ Employee satisfaction and workplace climate
- ▶ Assessment and information use

They also require the availability of information and evidence to determine and document outcomes and achievements in an objective manner for the benefit of the organization itself and for other constituencies.

Category 6 was concerned with establishing an assessment system that would permit the gathering and use of the information and evidence necessary to accomplish this goal. Category 7 focuses on the results that are obtained using this assessment system. Questions in this category relate to achievements and outcomes relative to each of the six dimensions of organizational efficiency described in previous categories.

7.0 OUTCOMES AND ACHIEVEMENTS: KEY REVIEW ISSUES

Category 7 considers *current outcomes* and *longer-term trends*. To place such efficiency outcomes and achievements in the most meaningful context, *comparisons* are also a topic of consideration. Comparisons allow a program, department or organization to determine how particular outcomes and achievements relate to those of peers, competitors or organizations that are considered leaders and models of excellence. Figures 15 through 21 provide illustration charts one can use to organize and present this kind of information.

FIGURE 15. 1.0 LEADERSHIP

EFFECTIVENESS INDICATORS (WHAT WE CURRENTLY MEASURE)	OUTCOMES FOR THIS YEAR (+/-/?)	COMPARED WITH PREVIOUS YEARS (+/-/FLAT/?)	COMPARED WITH PLANS AND GOALS (+/-/FLAT/?)	COMPARED WITH PEERS AND LEADERS (+/-/FLAT/?)
▸ ▸ ▸ ▸ ▸ ▸ ▸				
Wish List (what we should *ideally* measure)				
▸ ▸				

FIGURE 16. 2.0 STRATEGIC PLANNING

EFFECTIVENESS INDICATORS (WHAT WE CURRENTLY MEASURE)	OUTCOMES FOR THIS YEAR (+/-/?)	COMPARED WITH PREVIOUS YEARS (+/-/FLAT/?)	COMPARED WITH PLANS AND GOALS (+/-/FLAT/?)	COMPARED WITH PEERS AND LEADERS (+/-/FLAT/?)
▸ ▸ ▸ ▸ ▸ ▸ ▸				
Wish List (what we should *ideally* measure)				
▸ ▸				

FIGURE 17. 3.0 BENEFICIARIES AND CONSTITUENCIES

EFFECTIVENESS INDICATORS (WHAT WE CURRENTLY MEASURE)	OUTCOMES FOR THIS YEAR (+/-/?)	COMPARED WITH PREVIOUS YEARS (+/-/FLAT/?)	COMPARED WITH PLANS AND GOALS (+/-/FLAT/?)	COMPARED WITH PEERS AND LEADERS (+/-/FLAT/?)
Beneficiaries ▸ ▸ Constituencies ▸ ▸				
Wish List (what we should *ideally* measure)				
Beneficiaries ▸ ▸ Constituencies ▸ ▸				

FIGURE 18. 4.A PRODUCTS, PROGRAMS, SERVICES AND ASSOCIATED PROCESSES (MISSION-CRITICAL)

EFFECTIVENESS INDICATORS (WHAT WE CURRENTLY MEASURE)	OUTCOMES FOR THIS YEAR (+/-/?)	COMPARED WITH PREVIOUS YEARS (+/-/FLAT/?)	COMPARED WITH PLANS AND GOALS (+/-/FLAT/?)	COMPARED WITH PEERS AND LEADERS (+/-/FLAT/?)
▸ ▸ ▸ ▸ ▸ ▸ ▸				
Wish List (what we should *ideally* measure)				
▸ ▸				

FIGURE 19. 4.B OPERATIONAL AND SUPPORT SERVICES

EFFECTIVENESS INDICATORS (WHAT WE CURRENTLY MEASURE)	OUTCOMES FOR THIS YEAR (+/-/?)	COMPARED WITH PREVIOUS YEARS (+/-/FLAT/?)	COMPARED WITH PLANS AND GOALS (+/-/FLAT/?)	COMPARED WITH PEERS AND LEADERS (+/-/FLAT/?)
▶ ▶ ▶ ▶				
Wish List (what we should *ideally* measure)				
▶ ▶				

FIGURE 20. 5.0 EMPLOYEE SATISFACTION AND WORKPLACE CLIMATE

EFFECTIVENESS INDICATORS (WHAT WE CURRENTLY MEASURE)	OUTCOMES FOR THIS YEAR (+/-/?)	COMPARED WITH PREVIOUS YEARS (+/-/FLAT/?)	COMPARED WITH PLANS AND GOALS (+/-/FLAT/?)	COMPARED WITH PEERS AND LEADERS (+/-/FLAT/?)
Employee Satisfaction ▶ ▶ Workplace Climate ▶ ▶				
Wish List (what we should *ideally* measure)				
Employee Satisfaction ▶ ▶ Workplace Climate ▶ ▶				

FIGURE 21. 6.0 ASSESSMENT AND INFORMATION USE

EFFECTIVENESS INDICATORS (WHAT WE CURRENTLY MEASURE)	OUTCOMES FOR THIS YEAR (+/-/?)	COMPARED WITH PREVIOUS YEARS (+/-/FLAT/?)	COMPARED WITH PLANS AND GOALS (+/-/FLAT/?)	COMPARED WITH PEERS AND LEADERS (+/-/FLAT/?)
▸ ▸ ▸ ▸ ▸ ▸ ▸				
Wish List (what we should *ideally* measure)				
▸ ▸				

In summary, this category asks for the kind of information and evidence that allows a program, department or organization to determine, document and/or demonstrate where it stands now, over time and compared with other organizations. See Figure 22.

FIGURE 22. ACHIEVEMENTS COMPARISON

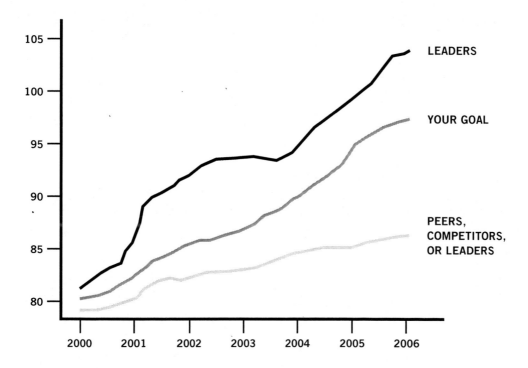

7.1 LEADERSHIP

1. What current and long-term outcomes and achievements are related to leadership effectiveness?[46]

2. How do these leadership outcomes and achievements compare with those of peers, competitors and/or leaders?[47]

7.2 STRATEGIC PLANNING

1. What current and long-term outcomes and achievements are related to strategic planning?

---

46 This category should present assessment results and evidence that document outcomes and achievements. The category does not consider information on your organization's approaches, intentions, strategies or methods. Those topics are the focus of Categories 1 through 6. Wherever possible, outcomes, achievements and progress (trends) should be presented in graphs and tables that display results in a clear and unambiguous manner.

Outcomes and achievements related to leadership should be based on measures and indicators established by your unit, as discussed in Category 6.

47 Comparisons should relate your outcomes and achievements to those of peers, competitors and/or leaders, as discussed in Category 6. Wherever possible, comparison information should be presented in graphs and tables that display results in a clear and unambiguous manner.

2. How do these strategic planning outcomes and achievements compare with those of peers, competitors and/or leaders?

7.3 BENEFICIARIES AND CONSTITUENCIES

1. What are the documented outcomes and achievements related to your relationship with beneficiary and constituency groups?

2. How do these outcomes and achievements compare with those of peers, competitors and/or leaders?

7.4 PRODUCTS, PROGRAMS, SERVICES AND ASSOCIATED PROCESSES

A. Mission-Critical Products, Programs, Services and Associated Processes

  1. What current and long-term outcomes and achievements are related to mission-critical products, programs and services, and their associated processes?

  2. How do these outcomes and achievements compare with those of peers, competitors and/or leaders?

B. Operational and Support Services and Associated Processes

  1. What current and long-term outcomes and achievements are related to the effectiveness and efficiency of important operational and support services and their associated processes?

  2. How do these outcomes and achievements compare with those of peers, competitors and/or leaders?

7.5 EMPLOYEE SATISFACTION AND WORKPLACE CLIMATE

1. What current and long-term outcomes and achievements are related to employee satisfaction and workplace climate?

2. How do these outcomes and achievements compare with those of peers, competitors and/or leaders?

7.6 ASSESSMENT AND INFORMATION USE

1. What current and long-term outcomes and achievements are related to the effectiveness of assessment and information-sharing approaches, methods and practices?

2. How do these outcomes and achievements compare with those of peers, competitors and/or leaders?

WORKS CITED AND SUGGESTED READINGS

Baldrige National Quality Program. (2006). *The 2006 criteria for performance excellence in business.* Washington, D.C.: National Institute of Standards and Technology. Accessed at *http://baldrige.nist.gov/Criteria.htm.*

Bennis, W. (1997). *Managing people is like herding cats.* Provo, Utah: Executive Excellence Publishing.

Brancato, C.K. (1995). *New corporate performance measures.* New York: The Conference Board.

Calhoun, J. M. (2002). Using the Baldrige criteria to manage and assess the performance of your organization. *The Journal for Quality & Participation, 25*(2), 45–53.

Collins, J.C. (2001). *Good to great.* New York City: Harper Collins.

D'Aprix, R. (1996). *Communicating for change.* San Francisco, California: Jossey-Bass Publishers.

Gayeski, D. (2007). *Managing the communication function: A blueprint for organizational success* (2nd ed.). San Francisco, California: IABC.

Heaphy, M. S., & **Gruska**, G. F. (1995). *The Malcolm Baldrige national quality award: A yardstick for quality growth.* Reading, Massachusetts: Addison-Wesley Publishing Company.

Hettinger, M. & **Hattori**, T., ABC. (2006). *Strategic planning: Your roadmap to success!* Presentation at the 2006 Leadership Institute, Charlotte, North Carolina. Available online at *http://www.iabc.com/leaders/pdf/2006LIstratcommplan.ppt.*

IABC. (2007). Code of ethics for professional communicators. Retrieved from *http://www.iabc.com/about/code.htm.*

Kaplan, R.S. & **Norton**, D.P. (1996). *The balanced scorecard.* Cambridge, Massachusetts: Harvard Business School.

Kaplan, R.S. & **Norton**, D.P. (2001). *The strategy-focused organization.* Cambridge, Massachusetts: Harvard Business School.

Kouzes, J.M. & **Posner**, B.Z. (1995). *The leadership challenge.* San Francisco, California: Jossey-Bass.

Middle States Commission on Higher Education. (2002). *Characteristics of excellence in higher education eligibility requirements and standards for accreditation.* Philadelphia, Pennsylvania: Middle States Commission on Higher Education.

Middle States Commission on Higher Education. (2003a). *Resources for student learning assessment.* Philadelphia, Pennsylvania: Middle States Commission on Higher Education.

Middle States Commission on Higher Education. (2003b). *Student learning assessment: Options and resources.* Philadelphia, Pennsylvania: Middle States Commission on Higher Education.

National Institute of Standards and Technology (NIST). (February 2006). Baldrige National Quality Program: home page. Retrieved from *www.quality.nist.gov.*

Potter, L. (1999). Strategic management and communication. In A. Wann (Ed.), *Inside organizational communication* (3rd ed.) (pp. 11–24). San Francisco, California: IABC.

Potter, L. (2001). *The communication plan: The heart of strategic communication* (2nd ed.). San Francisco, California: IABC.

Przasnyski, Z. & **Tai**, L. S. (2002). Stock performance of Malcolm Baldrige National Quality Award winning companies. *Total Quality Management, 13*(4), 475–488.

Ruben, B.D. (1995). The quality approach in higher education: Context and concepts for change. In B.D. Ruben (Ed.), *Quality in higher education* (1–35). New Brunswick, New Jersey: Transaction.

Ruben, B.D. (2004). *Pursuing excellence in higher education: Eight fundamental challenges.* San Francisco, California: Jossey-Bass.

Ruben, B.D. (2006a). *What leaders need to know and do: A leadership competencies scorecard.* Washington, D.C.: National Association of College and University Business Officers.

Ruben, B.D. (2006b). *The leadership style inventory: Becoming a strategic leader.* Washington, D.C.: National Association of College and University Business Officers.

Shaffer, J. (2000). *The leadership solution.* New York City: McGraw-Hill.

Sinickas, A. D. (1999). Communication research. In A. Wann (Ed.), *Inside organizational communication.* (3rd ed.) (pp. 31–57). San Francisco, California: IABC.

Suskie, L. (2004). *Assessing student learning.* Bolton, Massachusetts: Anker.

Tromp, S.A., **Ruben**, B.D. (2004). *Strategic planning in higher education: A leader's guide.* Washington, D.C.: National Association of College and University Business Officers.

Unseem, M. (1998). *The leadership moment.* New York City: Random House.

Vokurka, R. J. (2001). The Baldrige at 14. *Journal for Quality and Participation, 24*(2), 13–19.

Wann, A. (Ed.). (1999). *Inside organizational communication* (3rd ed.) San Francisco, CA: IABC.

GLOSSARY

Achievements – Results, accomplishments or outcomes.

Action Plans – Specific activities and steps taken as part of short- and long-term strategic planning. Through action plan development, general strategies and goals are made specific so that effective implementation is possible and probable.

Alignment – Consistency and synchronization of plans, processes, actions, information and decisions among units to support key unit- and organizationwide goals. Effective alignment requires a shared understanding of purposes and goals and the use of complementary measures and information to enable planning, tracking, analysis and improvement at the organizational, departmental, work group and individual level.

Approach – The methods and strategies used by an organization. Categories 1 through 6 focus on approach along with implementation.

Assessment – Most generally, a process of reviewing the approaches, implementation strategies, and outcomes of the activities of a program, department or organization. In this sense, the entire *Core Communication* model is an assessment approach. More specifically, assessment is the process of comparing outcomes against particular product, program or service goals to evaluate and improve those products, programs and services as well as associated processes. This narrow definition is the focus in Category 6.

Benchmarking – Establishing benchmarks—also termed *comparisons*—refers to the process of identifying, selecting and systematically comparing the organization's performance, activities, products, programs, services, processes, achievements and/or impact with those of other organizations. Comparisons may be with peer, competitor and/or leading institutions, or with organizations in other sectors with similar processes or activities.

Beneficiaries – Stakeholders, consumers, clients, publics, users, constituencies or customers for whom the organization undertakes activities or provides products, programs or services. The product, program or service will vary depending on the mission of the organization.

Collaborators – External groups or organizations with which the unit must coordinate to carry out its mission-critical work. Includes partnerships, alliances, professional groups and vendor-supplier relationships.

Comparisons – Establishing comparisons—also termed *benchmarking*—refers to the process of identifying, selecting and systematically comparing the organization's performance, products, programs, services, processes, achievements and/or impact with those of other organizations. Comparisons may be with peer, competitor and/or leading institutions or with organizations in other sectors with similar processes or activities.

Coordination – Alignment and synchronization of plans, processes, actions, information and decisions throughout an organization, department or program. Effective alignment requires a shared understanding of purposes and goals and the use of complementary measures and information to enable planning, tracking, analysis and improvement at the organizational, departmental, work group and individual level.

Cycle Time – The time required to fulfill commitments or to complete tasks.

Dashboard Performance Indicators – A set of performance measures or indicators—sometimes referred to as a *scorecard*—that summarizes all areas of organizational functioning identified as essential to assessing organizational effectiveness.

Effectiveness – Success in achieving an intended purpose.

Efficiency – Economies relative to time, money and resources.

Employees – Refers to all employee groups, including full- and part-time, as well as temporary employees.

Goals – High-level targets or end points that are sufficiently specific to allow for progress to be assessed and a determination to be made when they have been achieved. "Stretch" goals are selected to challenge the organization to greater performance than might otherwise be sought.

Groups and Organizations Served – Beneficiaries, stakeholders, consumers, clients, publics, users, constituencies or customers for whom the organization undertakes activities or provides products, programs or services. The product, program or service will vary depending on the mission of the organization.

Implementation – The manner in which approaches are deployed and applied within the organization.

Knowledge Utilization – Effective dissemination, sharing and use of information, expertise and knowledge by members of an organization.

Leadership System – The exercise of leadership and governance, formally and informally, throughout the organization; the way decisions are made, communicated and carried out. It includes structures and mechanisms for decision making, selection and development of leaders, and reinforcement of organizational values and practices. An effective leadership system creates clear values and high expectations for performance and improvement and monitors outcomes. It builds loyalties and teamwork based on the values and the pursuit of shared purposes. It encourages and supports initiative and avoids chains of command that require long decision paths. An effective leadership and governance system also includes mechanisms for the leaders' self-examination.

Mission – The primary work of the unit, the purposes for which the unit exists, is often published and made available to members of the organization and beyond.

Mission-Critical Products, Programs, Services and Associated Processes – Sequences of work activities that are mission critical; those essential to the organization's mission and its activities, products, programs and services.

Organization – The terms *organization, department, program* and *unit* are used interchangeably in *Core Communication*. The framework is equally applicable to an entire organization, a program, or a department.

Outcomes – Documented evidence of the organization's current accomplishments and achievements and performance over time relative to its mission, vision, values, goals and plans, including the quality, effectiveness and efficiency of leadership practices; planning processes; relationships with the beneficiary and constituency groups and organizations; products, programs, services and associated processes; employee satisfaction and workplace climate; and assessment and information use approaches.

Overview – The summary of an organization's major products, programs and services; its structure and key relationships; major recommendations from previous external or internal assessments; key challenges and opportunities; peers and/or competitors; and other information that is important to understanding the context in which the organization operates. The information is assembled as a part of the preparation for an assessment.

Performance – Refers to output and results. Performance information permits evaluation relative to goals, standards, past results, and the accomplishments of peer and other organizations.

Performance Measures – Measures or indicators of organizational functioning identified by a unit as appropriate for assessing organizational outcomes and achievement levels. Measures would typically include indicators of achievement relative to the mission, vision, values, goals and plans, and the quality, effectiveness and efficiency of leadership practices; planning processes; relationships with the beneficiary and constituency groups and organizations; products, programs, services and associated processes; employee satisfaction and workplace climate; and assessment and information use approaches.

Process – A sequence of activities. Processes include combinations of people, machines, tools, techniques and materials in a systematic series of steps, actions or activities.

Recognition – Methods for acknowledging the contributions of individuals, groups or work units. Recognition includes but is not limited to public acknowledgment of individuals and groups or teams, personal feedback, and merit awards. Also included are letters of commendation, certifications of merit, articles in bulletins or newsletters, announcements at unit meetings, and so on.

Results – The outcomes and achievements of an organization, department or program.

Service Standards – Organizational practices implemented to address identified needs and expectations of groups being served. They apply to those processes and people with direct contact with those external groups. Examples might include standards regarding call-back response time, response time to inquiries, wait times or telephone-answering protocol.

Stakeholders – Sometimes termed beneficiaries, external groups, consumers, clients, publics, users, constituencies or customers, stakeholders are those individuals or groups who influence and are influenced by the organization. They include those whose assessments are critical to the support and reputation of the organization.

Suppliers and Collaborators – Groups or organizations with which an organization collaborates that provide capital, material or human resources necessary for an organization, department or program to fulfill its mission. Alliance, partner and supplier relationships may exist with other departments in the organizations, such as human resources, marketing, customer service or accounting. They may also exist with external organizations, such as professional associations. Other examples are vendors of various types that supply goods and services.

Support Services – Sequences of activities necessary to the completion of mission-critical work and to the effective and efficient operation of the organization. Often, these processes are invisible to external groups. For example, organizational processes would include recruiting and hiring, conducting performance reviews, preparing budgets, training, purchasing equipment and supplies, coordinating repairs and maintenance, time and room scheduling, preparing work materials, and scheduling and conducting meetings.

Synchronization – Alignment and coordination of plans, processes, actions, information and decisions throughout an organization, department or program. Effective synchronization requires a shared understanding of purposes and goals and use of complementary measures and information to enable planning, tracking, analysis and improvement at the organizational, unit, work group and individual level.

Vision – A characterization of how the organization, department or program sees itself in the future—its broadly expressed aspirations.

ABOUT THE AUTHORS

Brent Ruben, Ph.D., is Professor II of communication and the executive director of the Center for Organizational Development and Leadership at Rutgers University. He conducts research, teaches, publishes, and provides professional consultation nationally and internationally in the areas of communication and higher education leadership and assessment, planning and continuous improvement. His recent books include: *A Guide to Excellence in Higher Education 2007-08: An Integrated Approach to Assessment, Planning, and Improvement in Colleges and Universities* (National Association of College and University Business Officers—NACUBO, 2007); *What Leaders Need to Know and Do* (NACUBO, 2006); *Communication and Human Behavior. Fifth Edition* (with L. Stewart, Allyn-Bacon, 2006); and *Pursuing Excellence in Higher Education: Eight Fundamental Challenges* (Jossey-Bass, 2004). Dr. Ruben is author of some 40 books and 200 book chapters and articles.

Dr. Ruben was the first president of the National Consortium for Continuous Improvement in Higher Education (NCCI), a member of the 2007 USDE Accreditation Regulations Negotiation Team, an examiner for the Department of Commerce/NIST Malcolm Baldrige National Quality Awards, and a member of the NIST Education and Healthcare Baldrige Pilot Advisory and Evaluation Team. He is the 2006 recipient of the Brent D. Ruben Award for distinguished contribution to higher education, created in his honor by the National Consortium for Continuous Improvement in Higher Education (NCCI). He is also the 2004 recipient of the National Communication Association Gerald Phillips Award for Distinguished Applied Scholarship. He has received the National Association of College and University Business Officers Professional Development and Scholarship Award (2003) and the Rutgers University Daniel Gorenstein Memorial Award for outstanding scholarship and service to the university community (2000). Dr. Ruben consults widely in higher education, health care, government and business.

Stacy Smulowitz, ABC, is president of Smulowitz Communications, a communication consulting firm specializing in public relations, web site development and design, employee communication, marketing, special events, and strategic planning.

Smulowitz is a Ph.D. student in communication at Rutgers University, where her studies focus on theory and strategy for assessing and promoting excellence in organizational leadership. She also holds an MA from Ithaca College in corporate communications. Stacy is past president of the International Association of Business Communicators (IABC) Lehigh Valley regional chapter.

0 1341 1387878 6